FROM SKINNY TO ALL BOOBS & ASS

A 4 Decade Love Story

Jennifer Belyea Ashe

Copyright © 2020 Jennifer Belyea Ashe

All rights reserved

No part of this book may be reproduced, or stored in a retrieval system, or transmitted in any form or by any means, electronic, mechanical, photocopying, recording, or otherwise, without express written permission of the publisher.

ISBN: 978-0-9813269-9-3
Publisher: Jennifer Belyea Ashe

For all the women who never felt their bodies were enough.

*For my husband and our children, who helped me
fully understand that I was enough all along.*

CONTENTS

Title Page	1
Copyright	2
Dedication	3
Preface	7
A Love Story	13
From Skinny…	18
Tortured Teen Years	23
University- The Dark Place	31
Denial and Pregnancy Pounds	39
My Days As a Dairy Cow	44
Deflated	50
Things May Not Be As They Seem	53
Hair Envy Led to Disaster	56
Mid-Life Dating and the Perfect Cookie	65
Repartnering With Just the Right Recipe	73
Forty-Three	80
The Wedding Dress – Part One	86
The Wedding Dress – Part Two	90
Dress Codes and Scandalous Titties	95
Thoughts in the Dental Chair	102

Shopping: Trusting the Sales Associate	104
Shopping: The Bounce Test	111
Shopping: Justifications and Excuses	114
I Do Not Wear Short Shorts	117
Raising Daughters	124
Legs, Pits and Lady Bits	128
Scales Measure Weight, not Happiness	131
Social Media Spies and Social Media Size	135
How Do My Jibbies Smell?	146
Seeing Brown	156
A Familiar Stranger	162
About The Author	167

PREFACE

I had no plans of writing a book. Well, not a book of such a personal nature anyway. During my adult years I had written and published a number of articles and professional resources, but writing an actual full-length book seemed like a huge, impossible endeavour for busy me. But one day, an unexpected thought sparked in my mind. Then and there I knew that I was to write an article about how I- a woman in my 40's- have worked to reconcile the ever-evolving feelings I have about my body. It would be relatable and articulate the painful process that so many other women have also navigated.

On that day of the spark, I had struggled once again with my clothing not fitting me properly. When I (for the umpteenth time) said to my partner that I had become "all boobs and ass" I knew there was something I needed to capture. It also sounded like a great title for an article.

As I started jotting down notes I surprised myself with how many experiences over my lifetime that I could remember that contributed to the way I felt in my 40's about my body. As I continued to brainstorm content rather effortlessly, my idea for an article became a short story, then grew to be its own book.

Let's think about this for a moment: *How concerning is it that I can write an entire book based on insecurities I have had about my body? And how concerning is it that I'm only one of countless women to share these insecurities?*

That's pretty darn concerning.

※ ※ ※

If I were to describe myself at this moment in time (age 44) in complete unveiled honesty, I could confidently state that I am a loving, creative, passionate, open-minded, altruistic, fair, resilient, resourceful, dedicated person, and am a good mom and partner. I would also dare to describe myself as accomplished. I define this accomplishment not by my career, by money earned, or because of things I own, but because of what I've done in my life that fits my core values and sense of purpose. I certainly have not had an easy life by any means, and I impress even myself when I think of what I've been able to do. They're small, personal victories, but I'm very proud of myself for them nonetheless. Let's just say the deck generally hasn't been stacked in my favour, so I've had to learn to play really good card hands. My resilience is one of my most appreciated qualities.

I also have attributes of which I am less celebratory. I struggle with depression and anxiety. I feel things too strongly sometimes. I can be forgetful and also get distracted. I tend to withdraw when things are difficult. I can take on too much (which is sometimes out of my control). I can have difficulty communicating in tense situations, especially verbally. I often don't feel my worth. I've had to work very hard at managing things like frustration and being too hard on myself.

I'm also proud of myself in regards to these "negative" attributes. I have worked tirelessly at managing these, much out of respect to my loved ones and thus trying to make myself more tolerable to live with. I've also worked on them for *myself*, and am proud of my personal growth over the years.

I haven't always been kind when evaluating my own physical attributes. I have come to realize with age that looks are less important, and what really matters is that the people I love the most see the beauty within me. I've learned to surround myself with good people who love me, and I know undoubtedly that I've accomplished that.

Like many young women, I was unsatisfied with the way I looked and was very self-critical. I was never one to vocalize these critiques though, so they remained in my head as negative self-talk, which spared others from having to listen to me gripe about this deep unhappiness. In fact, most people probably didn't know that I felt this way. On some level I didn't feel the right to outwardly complain, because I knew there were many who had more significant struggles with things like their weight than I did.

By the time I reached 40 years old I had grown a respectable level of confidence and self-acceptance and I was very embracing of my physical body. I had made incredible progress in being happy with myself. However, I was dealt a bad hand again, which made it more of a challenge to accept my body. That hand was chronic health issues.

Those with a chronic health condition can attest to how much it impacts their lives. Aside from the depression and anxiety that usually rear their ugly heads, there are great physical considerations that can be limiting. Pain can make it difficult to get exercise or do simple things like engage in basic self-care or clean your home. Many health conditions come with forms of muscle or joint weakness. Some people lose energy due to lack of sleep or nutritional complications. This just lightly touches the surface of what chronic health sufferers face and how their lives are impacted.

While I was going to physical therapy, my well-meaning physiotherapist kept nudging me towards finding a formal source of exercise. I appreciated why she was focused on this. She was encouraging me to keep moving, regain strength, and find a positive outlet.

While I respect her professional opinion, there were times I knew her encouraging was futile: when a person is struggling to get out of bed, the last thing they want to do is exercise. Here's the thing (this relates to Spoons Theory, which if you haven't heard of, you probably haven't become part of the online chronic health/disability support community, which is a very good thing): When you have a chronic health condition, you have a limited amount of energy. If you use it up, you don't get more until your body has had time to recover (sleep, rest, chocolate-covered almonds). Even when it does recover, you have no idea how much energy you will actually get back. It's kind of like having a power cord that shorts out sometimes and doesn't work effectively, despite being plugged in. It might take a week to get back to 68% battery capacity.

If your computer only gets partially charged, are you going to use the limited battery power to watch the new season of your favourite Netflix series, or are you going to waste it on playing Bejeweled in endless mode, with no end result?

That's right- Netflix will always win out.

The last thing I want to do when I have a partially charged battery is to use it all up going for a swim, as was the physiotherapist's suggestion. Sure, it feels quite nice to float in the pool, but there's no end accomplishment- I'm not swimming anywhere. There are no chocolate-covered almonds at the end of the swimming lane.

I tried, I really did. And when I'm feeling well enough, I usually try to share that energy with my partner by going for a long walk through the woods or on a trail. I didn't want to ignore her advice to get some solo exercise, but...

"My exercise is cleaning the house," I told her.

"Yes," she responded. "But I'm sure you still don't get enough steps in when you're doing that."

Oh, I beg to differ. There are 7 people, 2 cats, 1 rambunctious dog and 5 plants (2 living, 3 dead) in our house. So, when I'm housecleaning, it can definitely count as exercise, especially when picking up things off the floor and relocating them to their appropriate rooms all over the house.

The thing about choosing to clean over having a swim- if I clean, my stress level is much more manageable because things are organized in my living space. In my case, like for so many others, clearing the clutter in the home can help clear the clutter in my mind.

Maybe I'll take before and after photos to my next physio session, so she can see that I have a valid point.

A few years ago, I was at the height of my "intractable neck pain" which rendered me pretty much useless for quite some time. My daily goal at that time became getting up out of bed, making 5 lunches for school, plus doing the morning routine with my (disabled) son. Being able to do that was a huge deal. My daily goals also included very basic cleaning and prepping supper. I was surprised at how grateful I became to be able to prepare food and provide for my family, despite being home and unable to work.

So, with chronic pain, you do what you gotta do. You're often in survival mode. And swimming isn't part of it, unless you're being actively chased by a shark.

With not being able to exercise and be as physical as I once was, I began to notice it taking a toll on my shape. Unfortunately I also had aging and a slowing metabolism working against me. I'm losing muscle mass as I age and because of my chronic disorder. My very complex condition also wreaks havoc on my digestive system. With it not responding like it used to, I'm left with the undesired side effect of bloating, pain and weight gain.

This has been challenging for me. While I've learned to accept my body in many ways, having these symptoms has been unquestionably difficult. Clothing doesn't fit right. I'm uncomfortable or in pain- all of the time. I have little control over these things. In a way, I feel like I'm a thinner person, trapped in a deceptive chubbier body. It's hard to admit that these things are out of my control, and frankly I don't want them to be. I suppose this is why the need to write this book has emerged now, as I make sense of things.

A couple of lessons I would like to share:

Stay out of shark infested waters.

If you keep losing at cards, partner up with someone who has a better deck.

A LOVE STORY

This is a love story.

It's not your typical love story. It's definitely not a fairy tale love story. There's no man (or woman) coming to sweep me off my feet or to save me from malicious forces. Truth be told, the "saving" wouldn't be from the outside world, but rather, from myself.

You might be surprised that I'm even daring to categorize this as such. Really, it is a story about my journey of self-acceptance (and some self-loathing) that I've been on for quite some time now. One might be surprised that a story which includes self-loathing could also be a love story. It is. I'm choosing for it to be.

Identifying as a woman, my experiences and thought processes (thus, the "meat" for this book) will be that which I consider to be from a female perspective.

This is not to say that men do not have insecurities about their bodies or deal with outside influences that affect their self-view. In fact, writing this led to some very insightful conversations with my partner from his male perspective. I would speculate though that much of what we females focus on isn't equivalent to typical male physical insecurities. When one identifies as a specific gender (whether they were physically such at birth), with that comes the social construct of what that gender should look like, which then dictates the messages we get bombarded with and struggle with internally.

It's ironic, how much the internal and external can work against each other. Parts of a whole, in perpetual conflict for some.

Much of how women feel about their bodies could fall into what we would sadly categorize today as "normal." We are constantly bombarded with messages about how we should look- what size, what weight, how perky, how to dress to accentuate or hide what we have, how to alter our appearance with cosmetics and hairstyles, when to have cosmetic surgery. Even the slightest ill-comment can lead to a lifetime of detriment, yet we face a multitude of such ill-comments over our lives.

These messages come to us through traditional media, social media, peers, family, partners, close friends, even medical professionals. Retailers endlessly feed our insecurities and push messages onto us in an attempt to get us to buy their product or service. And they don't just attempt- they succeed. We can fruitlessly try to limit our exposure to these messages but there is no way of escaping them completely in today's world. The best tool we have as consumers is to become aware of how those (sometimes incredibly subtle) messages are influencing us.

Unfortunately, there are those who fall very deep into this cycle of self-loathing in relation to their weight or size, or with other things relating to their appearance. They can go on to develop eating disorders and other complex conditions like body dysmorphia. Although these disorders can be influenced and worsened by media and other social factors, they are deeply psychological, compulsive and addictive in nature. They become more about a loss of self and filling a void than about weight or size. The treatment for these conditions is not as simple as learning to love one's body and accept the natural aging process we all go through. Recovery from an eating disorder is a difficult process; anyone who is battling an eating disorder should work closely with health care professionals who specialize in this area.

If you have an active eating disorder, this book is not for you. These musings will not be relatable or helpful to those who are currently in that place. If you struggle with an eating disorder or suspect that you may (or be at risk), please speak with your doctor or other mental health practitioner. I am including some contact information at the end of this chapter. I highly encourage you to take this step. It is possible to feel better, and you are worth it.

If you are just trying to get through bathing suit shopping without crying in the changing room, or are just curious about what goes through my brain, this book is for you. Hang on for the ride!

As much as I hate to admit it, my body is changing. It's going to continue going through changes. Life plays funny tricks on you... you get to the point of self-acceptance, then – BOOM! you change because you keep aging. I guess I'm one of bazillions of people who doesn't accept change well.

At this rate, you can expect that I will be authoring a trilogy. Book #2 might be titled "No Longer Skinny, and My Boobs Hang Low." Book #3 might be titled "Chunky, But I'm Too Old to Care."

I'm typically a private person when it comes to anything personal. I have discussed my history and insecurities with very, very few people, and not in much detail. Sharing in this way makes me feel extremely vulnerable. Like being naked in a soccer field, spectators all around, and having nowhere to hide. That kind of vulnerable.

So, please close this book and don't read any further.
No, seriously.

* * *

If you have an eating disorder or suspect you might, please consider contacting the organizations below. In addition, you should talk to your family doctor. If starting that conversation is difficult, you may wish to print a resource to take with you.

Canada
National Eating Disorder Information Centre (NEDIC)
https://nedic.ca
Provides information, resources, referrals and support to Canadians affected by eating disorders.
Toll-free hotline: 1-866-633-4220

Canadian Mental Health Association
https://cmha.ca
(check your area for your local chapter)

* * *

United States
National Association of Anorexia Nervosa and Associated Disorders
https://anad.org
Currently serving people in the United States. Trained hotline volunteers offer encouragement to those having problems around eating or binging, support for those who "need help getting through a meal," and assistance to family members who have concerns that their loved one might have an eating disorder.
1-630-577-1330

National Eating Disorders Association (NEDA)
www.nationaleatingdisorders.org
The National Eating Disorders Association (NEDA) is the largest non-profit organization dedicated to supporting individuals and families affected by eating disorders. NEDA supports individuals and families affected by eating disorders, and serves as a catalyst for prevention, cures and access to quality care. Toll-free, confidential helpline.
1-800-931-2237

UK

National Centre for Eating Disorders
https://eating-disorders.org.uk
Eating disorder treatment and recovery (personal counselling), professional training courses in eating disorders, help for carers, information. Phone, in-person and Skype counselling.
0845 838 2040

Beat Eating Disorders, UK
https://www.beateatingdisorders.org.uk
Hotlines, and support for family and carers, information and resources, helplines, support groups. Peer coaching.
Helpline 0808 801 0677
Youthline 0808 801 0711
Studentline 0808 801 0811

* * *

Note: If you are looking online for eating disorder help or information, please make sure to look for a registered organization. Reputable organizations are mindful of triggers, such as photos and/or peer stories. Peer support can be valuable in recovery, but should be followed closely by a qualified medical professional.

FROM SKINNY...

I hate the word skinny. Hate it. That being said, it seems an unlikely word choice for a book that I'm titling, but there it is. SKINNY.

❋ ❋ ❋

I was nearly 10 lbs at birth. I know this detail because my mother has reminded me of this. A lot. But I figure she earned the right to complain or to announce her achievement.

I saw the baby pictures. I was a little chunky, chub of a baby, a round ball of pink. You can tell me apart from my brother in baby photos because not only was I more chubby, but I was from the generation that all clothes "for girls" were pink. If there's pink in the picture, it's me. I remember ruffles too. Cuz nothing else defines your gender better than ruffles on your clothing.

Note to self: buy my brother a pink, ruffled shirt for Christmas this year.

After I had passed my thunder thighs baby stage, I'm not sure what happened. Those early years are pretty fuzzy. I remember being ridiculously fussy when it came to food. I really didn't like many things. I had a sensitivity to certain textures, which prevented me from eating some foods. Unfortunately I wasn't consistent with my texture sensitivities, which I'm sure (rightfully) frustrated my parents. I'd eat hamburger one day... and not the next. Scrambled eggs was another food that I'd eat one day but not the next. I became brilliantly skilled at hiding those rubbery, greasy, disgusting breakfast sausages in my pockets with tissues, to later dispose of. Sometimes if our dog was lucky, I would manage to slip something I had deemed (humanly) inedible to him. To this day, I still cannot eat hamburger. I love the smell and I miss the taste. But, the texture of ground meat (of any kind) feels wrong in my mouth. My tongue amplifies the texture and I can't help but feel the little lumps and bumps, little pieces of gristle, and whatever else they throw in there. If I tried today, I'm pretty confident that I would not be able to swallow ground meat, despite the smell of it making me happily nostalgic.

My parents spent a good portion of my childhood just trying to get nutrition into me. I'm sure they deserve some kind of award for that. Obviously they succeeded because I am still here today.

I developed from a chub baby to a small child. I expect my petiteness was due to a mix of genetics and general lack of appetite. There wasn't much junk food in the house, so there wasn't much in that way to plump up on. My older brother was also a small child; I clearly remember him as a boy and teen, with his gangly legs, in his not-pink clothes. One of my favourite childhood photos is of young gangly-legged him holding out a frog for me, which I likely kissed. He used to get me to kiss frogs, none of which turned into a prince. I still love frogs. And my brother.

As a young child, I was aware that I was small, but many kids were back then. I didn't feel out of the ordinary.

Puberty was not my friend. In fact, it didn't make an appearance until what I would consider to be late. Unfortunately for me, I was one of those kids who really wanted to just fit in, not stand out. I didn't wear a bra yet. I didn't need a bra yet. But damn, I really wanted that bra. But, I also wanted to *need* the bra.

Had nature had the chance to progress on its own without judgement, I feel that things would have been different. I always felt the comparison of the other girls though. At that age,

I certainly didn't feel the desire to look like a woman. If I had just been left alone to do what my body was supposed to do, I wonder how things would have turned out differently. But no, I had things like puberty pamphlets cruelly pressuring me with timelines that outlined when I was supposed to start developing. I hated those pamphlets. I also hated the questions that were asked of me from other girls.

I remember being in class in junior high and the kids starting a conversation (not teacher led), asking what church each of us belonged to. By my observations, there didn't seem to be any one religion that was better than another. Eventually, the kids would corner me.

"What church do you go to?" they'd ask, their tone already filled with judgement.

Initially I'd say "none" which was met with disbelief and horror. They actually told me that because I hadn't been baptized or "ceremonied in" (however one is supposed to be ceremonied into to secure their future place in heaven) that I'd be going to hell. Since that time, I have worried that this was my fate.

That doesn't make any sense, I used to think. *How does a just God condemn an innocent child or young person who had no control over whether or not their parents had dunked them in water as an infant?*

I didn't understand how some of those jerks were going to the Promised Land in the afterlife, while I (a very nice, well-behaved child and good student) was not.

I eventually smartened up, like I very often do after much too long; when I was then asked the question about religion, I told them I was Baptist. This wasn't a complete lie. My father's parents were Baptist, so I figured I had earned part of that title by default. I had also attended Sunday school a few times with a friend, because they had fun activities for kids. Identifying as Baptist seemed to keep my peers content enough to stop telling me I was a cursed soul.

Well, my peers weren't any kinder when it came to puberty. Not only was I was going to hell, but I was going to hell *skinny*.

I felt so shamed by the girls in particular. I wonder now how much of that shame was amplified by my young mind. Maybe I thought they were being meaner than they were, or judging me more than they actually were. But in my pre-pubescent and very sensitive mind they were heavily judging me. They called me skinny. Skinny became a word that had a negative connotation to me. It was the judge-y way of saying someone is slender or slim. I always heard a level of disgust behind that word. I felt as though the judgement was mostly directed at me from the girls who were already developing curves.

There I was, skinny and vulnerable. I was most vulnerable during gym class, which I quickly learned to hate even more than I had before. I wasn't athletic. I wasn't popular. I was always next to last to get picked for teams. It was completely embarrassing.

Gym class is the education system's way of torturing awkward, underdeveloped non-athlete children. I'm not sure why they want to do this, but I insist that it must be true. Dodgeball is their way of further traumatizing the non-athletic children. There's no better way to bring children together than by giving aggressive kids permission to whip balls at timid kids. I still cower when I'm around a sport with flying balls, for fear of being hit. I wonder how many people went on to have PTSD due to gym class dodgeball games.

While clearly vulnerable in the gym during activities, I was most vulnerable in the changing room itself. We were required to change into and out of gym clothes. Changing in front of my developing peers exposed me to their looks and comments. Before gym class AND after gym class. Twice. I was painfully aware that the girls were wearing bras, and I wasn't. I'd modestly try to cover my body, especially where my breasts should be. I was too embarrassed to expose a bare nip.

At what exact point in her life does a girl decide she is too embarrassed to expose her nipple? Or rather, at what point does society decide that that girl can't expose her nipple?

The irony in this case- I wasn't embarrassed and covering because said nipple was on a breast; I was covering *because it was not*.

Eventually I did get a bra, and so I fit in in that sense. It was a good number of years though before a bra served a real purpose. Finding bras was a painful process even then. I was incredibly modest and hated the entire thing, especially when it involved a stranger measuring me for the right fit. Then I had to look at myself in the mirror to decide on the fit, something I still haven't quite figured out.

This is what really warps my mind when I think about it…

When I was that age, I would often walk to the beach with my friends. Sometimes we'd go swimming. Sometimes we'd just lay on the beach and hang out. Being much more modest than girls today, we wore huge oversized t-shirts over our bathing suits. Huge. This was the era that girls didn't wear anything fitted. Heck, we basically wore tents in junior high and high school. My friends would often remove their tent/t-shirts to go swimming. I rarely removed mine because I was too self-conscious about my body. Even then, at -45 lbs, I was self-conscious. And I remember thinking that I had a little "pot belly" and chubby thighs, which is comical to think about now. Luckily when I did venture into the water with my tent on, it didn't weigh me down to the point of no return.

There is little wonder that I later developed issues when I put on a little weight and changed size and shape.

TORTURED TEEN YEARS

When I was in elementary school, we were asked to draw a picture of ourselves in the career we would like to have when we were older. I decided that I was going to become a nurse. No, I didn't end up becoming a nurse, but it was something at the time I thought I wanted to be. I spent a ridiculously long time on that drawing.

Of course, I dressed myself in a dress. (As everyone knows, dresses are the most practical nursing attire. And, I was a girl, and that's what girls wore, right?) The skirt part of my dress had a nice flare. Not poofy or full like a crinolined skirt, and not restrictive like a pencil skirt. It was a nice in between.

In the drawing, I was walking from one very happy injured patient to another very happy injured patient. I appeared to be carrying a letter. Apparently I was a postal delivery nurse.

The most tedious part of that drawing (and where I spent the majority of my time) was trying to draw my breasts. I knew I would be a woman at that time and therefore have breasts, but I didn't know how to draw them. I struggled with giving them the right shape and have some dimension on paper. If my future nurse-self stood to the side, my breasts should jut out. But if I was standing facing front, how would I draw them properly? I spent an absurd amount of time trying to get this right, because I felt it was very important. I remember feeling quite strange about this change that would come to my body, but proud of it just the same.

My children now laugh at that drawing, because my boobs are way too close to my chin. I tried to convince them that such was the style in the 80's, but they didn't fall for it. My breasts were never that perky. I'm not sure anyone's were.

Fast forward to my high school years. Still no breasts. But breasts weren't the only thing I was missing. I was missing confidence. I was missing self-acceptance. I didn't know how to be proud of myself. I didn't realize how debilitating this was for me at that time. I brushed it off as shyness and anxiety, but it was so much more.

I'm not sure when I "officially" became clinically depressed, but it crept in in high school. I felt very lost. I didn't understand my value or my place in the world. I was extremely sensitive and at times over-empathic. I cried myself to sleep over the cruelties happening to people in other parts of the world (and closer to home) but felt completely helpless as a young person and felt that I was unable to make a real difference.

I had very few close friends in high school, but that was ok with me. I loved those few friends dearly. They accepted me for my quirky self, and I didn't feel the need to impress them. I steered away from the "popular" kids, and refused to care about popularity and things such as brand name clothes. Even then, I was a non-conformist in many ways. Because my goal was to lay low, I avoided being the target of bullying and ridicule. When I think back to the pretty bizarre games I played as a child, I'm not sure how I successfully evaded torment. Maybe the bullies were too scared of my weirdness to come close.

I was much too hard on myself in my teen years, which later came to haunt me. I was creative, and I loved any initiative that involved helping others. Even though I avoided the "popular" kids as best I could, I still often worked beside them. I was involved with various play committees (except for acting) and was very involved in my school, particularly grad year. During grad year I lost weight from my already petite frame. I believe when I graduated I weighed in at around 95 lbs. I no longer filled out the prom dress that was made for me. It hadn't been an intentional weight loss; I had been so busy and distracted with activities that I simply hadn't gotten as much nutrition as I probably should have. I recall being surprised by the weight loss, but not happy about it. I was indifferent.

While I was indifferent to the weight loss in grade 12, this soon changed. University brought with it a whole new set of pressures, challenges and expectations. I wasn't aware of how serious it would become, and how everything would build. When one's depression and need for control gets interwoven with one's perception of self and looks, it is a dangerous combination.

※ ※ ※

I couldn't fairly end the chapter there, since there was more teenage angst to report.

Let's talk about acne- everyone's favourite subject. Acne isn't usually given enough credit for its impact on the teenage psyche. Acne can paralyze a person who has social phobias and anxiety. The same has been said for other things that appear out of the "norm" on one's face (crooked teeth, other skin conditions, birthmarks, etc.). We can't hide our faces for comfort's sake since most of our communication happens in person. Well, it did before becoming so dependent on technology.

I was one of those unfortunate people who suffered from acne. As a bit of an aside, as a chronic health and disability advocate, I have made it a rule to not use the term "suffers from" when describing a person's condition. I can usually find a silver lining in even the poorest of situations. But, I'm really not sure anything good comes with acne. If someone knows of any, I encourage you to contact me and share some of that wisdom. So yes, I feel justified in using the word suffer.

Acne sucks.

I started to develop acne as a teenager, specific age unknown. Breakouts didn't help my already painful shyness. I became even more insecure about how I looked. It was probably around that time that I started experimenting with makeup. A cover stick became my best friend. Nearly 30 years later, it still is. The nature of our relationship has changed over the decades though; not only do I use it now to help cover breakouts, but also to cover the dark circles that have become permanent eye features.

In fact, if I could choose only one piece of makeup today, it would be a cover stick. I'm a wee bit envious of our youthful daughters who *may* apply a simple coat of mascara, then their makeup routine (if you can call it one) is done for the day. One of our daughters has such long and thick eyelashes that when she puts on mascara, her lashes become the envy of every woman and drag queen. I once applied mascara to her father's lashes to see if she got this trait from him, but the results suggested that she did not. Although, his eyes did look very pretty. Then again, they always do.

Eventually I did expand my makeup routine, but I was always faithful to my best friend, the cover stick. If I dared to leave the house for a quick errand… cover-up. I discovered that if I really wanted/needed to leave work early, I could just go to work with no makeup on. I'd look so tired and "ill" that there'd be no question about leaving early. (To my defense, I think I only ever did this twice, and I wasn't feeling well- to the point that I didn't feel like putting makeup on anyway.)

In university, I gained a bit more confidence, but face-to-face talk was still difficult for me. It was even more difficult when I was aware of a breakout. *Hey maybe it's just me, right? It's my face and I'm more aware of that pimple than others, right?*

And then one day (I was 18 or 19) I was home visiting a friend. Her boyfriend said to me "your face cleared up so much since you went to university." *WTF? Who says that to someone?!?? Was that supposed to be a compliment?!??* I don't remember what my response was, but I think I was too stunned to respond with a witty comment or physical violence. Obviously that comment stuck with me, all these years later.

My friend eventually broke up with that loser.

That sentence deserves emphasis.

MY FRIEND EVENTUALLY BROKE UP WITH THAT LOSER!

What I learned from that terrible experience is that some young (loser) men were paying attention to my skin. As such, I continued to be self-conscious about breakouts. I used to joke about how I'd later be in my 40's and be developing wrinkles but still have acne. Guess what??!? Nature can be a cruel thing.

My anti-love story with acne has been an on and off one for three decades now. When I was pregnant with my first child (a whole 20 years ago), I received a very thoughtful gift- a gift certificate for a massage. The person who had given it to me later asked if I had used it, but I hadn't. I couldn't tell them the truth and kept making excuses as to why I hadn't gotten the massage yet. The reason was because my back was broken out from the hormones and the thought of someone seeing it and touching me was very upsetting to me. Even though I still get breakouts today, I'll be damned if I'd let a little back acne keep me from getting a massage. I'd strip naked for anyone, with an enthusiastic "RUB ME!!!!"

Ok, I totally wouldn't do that for many reasons, but for my massage therapist, absolutely. Besides, they're professionals- they've dealt with this stuff many times. They don't get scared off by a little back acne.

Now in my 40's, makeup is still my crutch. It makes me feel fresher and put together, and more confident.

However, it's so darn time-consuming to "put on my face." As I've evolved, I've let go of needing makeup, even cover-up, when going to the grocery store. In fact, I'm editing this paragraph right now in a waiting room waiting for my daughter, looking like I threw myself together in 27 seconds (probably because I did). Which goes without saying, I have two distinct looks: really put-together or like I've been living on the street for a month. I don't need to impress anyone at this point, as I have the partner I want. If I'm shopping for groceries, the groceries don't seem to care about the ghoulish circles under my eyes.

One definite benefit to make up though... I've noticed that when I'm looking put-together I'm much more playful with my partner. He doesn't care if I wear makeup, as he's very much attracted to me without it. But if I'm feeling extra playful, then he kinda likes it. ;)

❊ ❊ ❊

I babysat a lot in my teen years. At one of my regular gigs, the little girl was playing with my long hair. She made a very innocent comment about my "sprinkles." She hadn't learned the word for dandruff yet. I stammered through some response and changed the subject. When I think about it now, sprinkles was a very cute way of phrasing it. That simple name change gave it almost a positive connotation... *would you like sprinkles with that? Sprinkles are always good, right?* However my teenage brain at that time was mortified, and it made me paranoid for a very long time.

Then there was the occasion that a friend and I were hanging out with some younger kids that my friend knew. On that day, they told me my nose was big. I honestly had not ever considered this before that point. That comment forever changed the way I perceived my own face. I started checking my profile with a hand mirror and a larger mirror, so I could see what others saw from other perspectives. I spent the next 20 years having great paranoia about my nose, envious of people with cute little noses, and secretly wishing I could have a nose job. There were times I thought that breaking my nose would be desirable, because maybe I could have it fixed and reshaped, smaller. I could not watch a movie without admiring a cute nose on an actress.

It wasn't until I had my own children that I realized that changing my nose would change my entire facial appearance.

The thought of wanting to change my appearance - the way they knew me - seemed ludicrous and unforgiveable. And the desire to change my nose stopped, just like that.

In time, I came to admire noses that are distinguished. Many people go through an awkward time before they grow into their nose. Some of those people are considered to be very attractive (try perusing through photos of actors). A nose provides a great amount of definition and character to one's face. How many times have I looked lovingly at my children's noses, all of which are so different? How many times have I run my finger down the nose of my partner, admiring his profile? I wouldn't change any of them. And I now wouldn't change mine.

I was also that kid who had to grow into their feet. I had large feet from a very early age, and it took awhile until tiny little me grew into my foot size. As a teenager, if I were shopping for footwear I would refuse to buy a shoe or boot over size 8 because I was so self-conscious about the size. It seems laughable to me now. I guess teenage girls did ask each other about sizes, but did it really matter in the grand scheme of things?

Would I go back to my teen years if I had the chance to do a do-over? Absolutely-frickin-no.

* * *

That little girl who commented on my sprinkles... she went on to get married and have three beautiful children of her own. She reached out to me via social media one day, sending me a message. It was sweet and (of course) made me cry. I guess my sprinkles had been the least memorable thing about me after all:

Hi, I have been meaning to write you. I wanted to say that I remember how much I looked up to you as a little girl and I thought you were so beautiful and I loved having you babysit us. I only get to see into a glimpse of your life now. I still look up to you. It seems like you are still an amazing person, a strong and independent person and still so pretty. You have such a beautiful family and I am sure they have the best mom. I just wanted to let you know.

UNIVERSITY- *THE DARK PLACE*

Like many young people, I was excited to go away to university and have the opportunity to spread my wings. I chose a school about an hour and a half from home; it was far enough to be away, but close enough I could get home to family and friends in an emergency or for a social call.

It was in university that I had my first boyfriend. Although I had had crushes in high school, I had been so painfully shy that they didn't go anywhere. At 18 I finally took the leap. (The "liquid courage" that I had made friends with that year helped me work through some of the shyness and speak to people.) The person I dated seemed safe. I was his first girlfriend. He was also shy and figuring things out. It was non-threatening. Like so many in their first relationship, I quickly got caught up in the puppy love of it.

Prior to living away from home, I didn't have access to junk food or fast food all the time. Growing up, those things were usually reserved for occasional weekend treats. Living away opened those doors for access. My (then) boyfriend and I made a regular habit of ordering garlic fingers from a nearby pizza place. We ordered so often in fact that they learned our voices and when we would call all we had to do was ask for our usual. Twenty minutes later, we would be scarfing down the most delicious garlic fingers in the universe.

The "usual"= 12" garlic fingers, real bacon bits and donair sauce.

Living in residence and eating in the cafeteria was a whole new thing for me. It was sometimes a difficult thing, because I was still rather picky when it came to food. But I could choose what I wanted, and we were pretty much unlimited with items. It was then that I discovered the beauty of breakfast. I had never been a breakfast eater prior to that time, but I became one for a few years. My roommate and I would drag ourselves out of bed late, often hungover (if we thought we could stomach food at that point). It was like a big, beautiful breakfast buffet.

I discovered I liked eggs, but only the egg whites. I'd get a fried egg and boiled egg, removing the yolks from both. There was bacon. I'd use the fun industrial toaster and toast up a half a bagel, loaded with cream cheese. And yogurt, so much yogurt. Sometimes I'd have very buttery toasted English muffins, toasted to perfection- not too light but not too dark. Then there were the fruit juices and chocolate milk. I loved those late breakfasts, with the exception of those disgusting greasy, aforementioned breakfast sausages. I couldn't sit at the same table as someone eating those sausages. Chewing on those is like gnawing on Satan's fingers. Nasty.

It was in the cafeteria in which I had a very profound realization about my size, or rather, my height. Before then, I had always thought I was very short. I was a bit self-conscious of that too, waiting to grow a bit more, but it never happened. But while standing in that cafeteria line I realized that I was looking other girls right in the eye. There were even girls who were shorter than me. Since then my height has been something I don't think much about.

Those buffet breakfasts really knew how to settle my stomach. They also, with the help of garlic fingers and excessive amounts of alcohol, knew how to pack on the pounds.

I guess most people have heard of the Freshman Fifteen -the widely accepted phenomenon that freshman gain around 15 lbs their first year of college. I was not immune to this phenomenon. When I went home to visit, not only did I bring with me a semester of courses and knowledge under my belt, but also breasts on my chest.

It shouldn't be any surprise that weight gain on an underweight female of 18 would put weight on where we are biologically designed to – breasts, bum, thighs. But I was not prepared for the changes at all. My breasts (although not large by any standard) got in the way of my arms. I wondered how women with larger breasts played sports. Or the cello. My filled-out bottom made it challenging to find jeans that fit properly. I didn't like the attention that my new body changes brought. I would describe my body type then as still slim, with curve.

The honeymoon period of that first relationship wore off and jealousy made its appearance, and stayed. An extremely jealous 19 year old male is never a good thing. To say he treated me badly would be an understatement. In hindsight, I should have ended things sooner, but I was young and naïve and broken and didn't know how to move forward. He also had a gift for turning things onto me, making me feel guilty and worthless. He was determined to make me believe that I couldn't be without him, and that other guys wouldn't want to be with me. I was scared to be with him, and scared to leave.

He also made references to my body and weight. Those stuck.

After the relationship had officially ended, he went into a lengthy mental breakdown phase. He avoided seeing me, shaved his head and withdrew. He later told me that he left the country and did something working with dead people (the details of which escape me). He accused me of being to blame for this breakdown, that I had driven him to these extremes and that I hadn't rescued him. "You didn't even notice," he accused.

I had noticed. In fact, everyone noticed. He made sure that it couldn't be overlooked by anyone. But I knew that me being involved would only make things worse for him, and for me. I did the right thing for both of us by keeping my distance.

My own post-breakup mental breakdown was not anywhere near as dramatic as his. In fact, I hid mine the best I could.

By that time, I was in *The Dark Place*.

After the breakup, I felt worthless and humiliated. I didn't trust men. I didn't want to get close to another person, or to get hurt again. Because I was terrified to enter into another relationship, I stayed single for the next few years of my life, my prime young dating years.

I was also dealing with other demons at the time and didn't know how to deal with them. I began to struggle immensely with my perception of myself (physically and otherwise). My need to find something to control settled on my marks and my weight. I rejected the normal healthy weight gain that had disrupted my earlier, slimmer sense of identity. I became obsessed with controlling this.

I liken having an eating disorder to having other kinds of addictions. It's compulsive and you're always in it. Many of the thought processes are the same. People who struggle with addiction are master hiders- they learn to hide from friends and family and others around them. They're protecting that at all costs. I didn't want help. I wanted to keep my secret. I would have died to keep that secret.

I could share with you the thoughts. How it was on my mind all of the time. *The Dark Place*. I could share with you all the things I did to hide. I can't. I can't go there. What I do want to share is that I was mentally tortured. Those years were torture for me. The fact that I made it through still surprises the hell out of me.

But, I didn't think I had a problem. I thought I had it under control. I was a smart person, it was under control. I thought I could stop if I needed to. It wasn't until I had suffered for years that I realized I didn't have it under control, and that I had an actual real, life-threatening issue. I struggled with acknowledging this and getting help because I was deeply ashamed.

I made an appointment with a counsellor on our university campus. I sat in the waiting room, riddled with anxiety. While I sat, I noticed a poster on the wall for a peer group meeting for people with eating disorders. I couldn't fathom revealing this to one person, let alone a group of people. I knew then and there that I would not be participating in that group.

I had made the assumption (even prior to the appointment) that the counsellor would be kind and approachable, which was helpful. She was married to one of my professors, whom I really liked. He would often tell stories about his family. They were both professionals, so they took each other's last names when they married. My feminist self thought that was really cool, as I had never heard of a man doing this.

When I got called into her office, I sat down across from her and tried to talk. Total failure. I cried. I didn't just cry, I sobbed. I was such a smart person. *How could I admit that I was harming myself? Smart people don't do these things*, or so I told myself. Of course, I know now that it is those (smart) perfectionist types that often develop poor coping skills like this. I know now that I should not feel shame in this. But at the time, I was too embarrassed to admit anything. I had been hiding for so long, and also wasn't sure I was ready to give up the control that I perceived I had.

I don't recall much of the first session because it was so long ago, and because I'm not quite sure I was even able to speak. I do remember discussing the guilt of peanut butter with her. So, I'm guessing I did finally reveal why I was there, rather than just blow her monthly Kleenex budget with my excessive crying.

Unfortunately, just after I began this counselling process, I was suddenly hit with a major illness. I was struggling to do anything and was not able to walk from my apartment to the counselling building. My days of seeing the counsellor came to an end too quick. I was still broken and hiding. What's worse is that I blamed myself for the health crisis I was then facing. I felt more guilt and shame. In time, with a lot of work and with future counselling, my unhealthy obsessive thoughts became more aligned with what the "average" woman faces. What I mean by this is that they became more self-critical and not an obsessive need to control. Still not healthy, but a heck of a lot more healthy than being in *The Dark Place*.

※ ※ ※

When I was around 19 years old, I had to have my tonsils out due to recurring infections. Because of my age I had to stay overnight in hospital. (Apparently there is much less risk and quicker recovery for a child from this surgery, and they considered me to no longer be a child.) At one point after the surgery, I vomited up the blood I had ingested. As much as I tried to keep it contained, I did not. (WHY are those little puke basins so small??) I back-splashed some lovely old blood vomit onto my sexy hospital gown.

I was mortified. I couldn't change myself and had to call a nurse. At this point in my life, I had very little experience with nurses, so I really didn't understand that blood or puke or boobs (or all three at once) would not phase a nurse. I was embarrassed because I had vomited on myself. I was also embarrassed about having a nurse see my bare chest.

Having been through a lot of medical procedures now in my 40's, I look back at that incident with amusement. But, I bet it's safe to say that many young women/teens are extremely modest of their recently developed chest and would feel strange in that situation.

※ ※ ※

I'd like to preface these next few paragraphs by saying that I'm going to make some very generalized statements about men and women. I certainly know that we do not all share the same beliefs or actions. I do not believe that all men objectify women. And there are women who will not share these observations. Gender (norms, behaviours, etc.) is very complicated, as are all things that are socially constructed.

It is a very strange time in a girl's life when she goes from not having anything (to hide) to being told that she has to cover up. It's when the curves come and the breasts come that others get uncomfortable with the attention that comes with it; she is then told to dress "appropriately." Breasts seem to be a visual reminder that human females are sexual beings, which parents (and others) can become very awkward about. Fathers can become uncomfortable with developing daughters because they know how men can think. Mothers can become uncomfortable with developing daughters because they have experienced harassment and unwanted attention from men after their own development. One could argue that a parent is trying to protect their daughter, but should she need to be protected from her own body, or what people are thinking about it?

As much as we try to accept female development as a natural process that should not be made shameful, we still send messages for females to cover. This is a very confusing way to live. Girls go from being not sexualized to being sexualized very quickly, usually much before she herself is ready to be seen in that light.

This all happened for me later than most because I was such a late bloomer. I recall being at the bar and having older men looking me up and down with that *look*. I'm guessing all grown women know the look I speak of. Well, it immediately made me feel dirty. I was an object. And not a pretty or smart or funny object that they were curious about... I was an object that served one purpose, and I didn't like it.

I doubt most men give it a second thought when they walk past a construction site, or other place in which a group of men are gathered together. How many times have I walked past construction workers and gotten the *look*. Sometimes there are comments accompanying the *look*. Even when there are no comments verbalized, I still FEEL the *look*.

There is a difference between a quick look where a woman has piqued someone's interest, and when men feel entitled to look at her like an object. If it were night at the time and not many people around, I would feel very unsafe and would avoid passing a group of males if I could. I would try to make myself unseen, invisible. And even if I don't feel physically unsafe, I can still feel unsettled.

This didn't happen before breasts and other curves.

It doesn't help that both sexes are taught mixed messages about these sorts of things. Some men think that women want attention (and indeed, some do in one capacity or another). They may think that a female is grateful that she is considered to be sexually attractive and someone is noticing. Therefore, a male may not even realize that a stare is making a female uncomfortable. And as girls who are developing, we are bombarded with messages that it's good to be able to capture the attention of males with our bodies. This can be a very tricky and often icky time for teenage girls.

Many women (this is common particularly of those who have experienced sexual trauma as a child or adult) resort to hiding their bodies with loose, unflattering clothing; they are trying to avoid attention from men. They feel like if they look less desirable and they disguise their shape, it will protect them. This is the world we live in.

Yes, there is a strong biological reason for men to be physically attracted to young women. Obviously we are meant to be attracted to each other for reproductive purposes and continuation of the species. The bodily changes we go through are a part of that. But damn, the unwelcome (sexual) attention from men and our loved ones (to cover up) can really, really mess around with one's personal perception of their developing body.

DENIAL AND PREGNANCY POUNDS

I credit having become a mother with saving my life. Having a wee one to support physically when I was pregnant persuaded me to focus on better physical health. It also motivated me to focus on my mental health. Luckily for me, my maternal survival instinct was very strong, and helped me face the demons that had been plaguing me. I also found a strong sense of purpose and identity after having children, which was key in my recovery.

❊ ❊ ❊

I was destined and designed to have children- no question of it. I was drawn to their unconditional love, their innocence, their curiosity... and I had a great desire to teach them key things about life. I just always knew, on every level, that I was meant to be a mother.

I often wonder if the childbirth videos that are shown to us in school are meant to scare us away from having children. This seems to have worked on at least one of my daughters, as she is adamant that she will be adopting her children. I likewise remember being traumatized by those videos.

No way I am doing that. I don't do well with pain. I would not survive childbirth. Not for me, nope. The act of making a baby is ICK. I will somehow miraculously conceive my own children, and avoid the process entirely.

Denial is a beautiful, beautiful thing.

In my youth, while I was completely uncomfortable with my peers and some adults, I was very comfortable with children. One of the qualities I love most about young children is their gift of being non-judgemental. A child will say what they are thinking. Sometimes this makes for an awkward situation, such as when they haven't yet learned what's considered socially acceptable (pointing out your sprinkles). It's easy to be understanding though when their intentions aren't bad. Their statements are driven by curiosity, not malice. It's a lot easier to recover from the perceived truth as told by a 5 year old than the perceived truth as told by a 15 year old.

Being comfortable around kids is one thing, but actually having my own is an entirely different thing.

First of all, I can't keep a plant alive. Even a cactus. Seriously.

If I can't keep plants alive, surely I wouldn't be able to help a child grow and thrive?

Secondly, having kids is scary. As I've already alluded to, the idea of a little human barrelling out of your vagina is terrifying.

What I also found terrifying was the weight gain that would come with having a baby. Before becoming pregnant, while I was oohing and ahhhing over all the sweet miniature shoes and onesies, I wasn't thinking about how I'd quadruple my weight over 9 months (ok, I don't think it was that bad, but it certainly felt like it). My deep desire for having children drowned out the petrified voice I had in my head that was telling me not to gain weight.

My first pregnancy was hell. I had severe morning sickness, at any and all times of the day. My "morning" sickness had been so bad that I had to tell people I was pregnant earlier than I would have liked (otherwise they thought I was contagious). My allergies acted up. I developed bronchitis, which turned into pneumonia. I had what was believed to be a pinched nerve (which shot excruciating pain down my leg when I walked). I had acid reflux so bad that on one occasion when I had to call in sick for work, I was unable to speak because the acid had burned my throat raw. My right hip slipped out of joint and was not only painful but greatly affected my mobility. I developed double ear infections. If you've ever had ear infections, especially two at once, I want you to imagine how difficult it would be to push out a baby, and the pressure you'd have in your head and ears doing so. It was not a good time to have double ear infections.

Prior to pregnancy, I had been a moderate bread eater. Yes, I did indulge in a fair amount of peanut butter and jam toast. But other than that, I didn't eat a lot of the white, nutrition-less stuff. I had always been very fond of fruits and vegetables, so my diet had been fairly healthy. But during my pregnancy when my guts turned to a vat of acid, I couldn't tolerate fruit. The only thing I could tolerate somewhat was bread. If I didn't have something in my belly (of a bread nature), I would vomit.

My (then) husband kept me fed by bringing me a lot of tuna sandwiches from our local coffee shop. I ate an embarrassing amount of tuna sandwiches. (They likely had to hire extra employees that year because of all the business I gave them.) I wasn't eating the sandwiches due to a pregnancy craving...it was an aversion to everything else. It's surprising that tuna didn't turn my stomach, but it didn't. The other thing I consumed a lot of at that time was bagels. And crackers. Oh, so many crackers...

I went to my family doctor very early in my pregnancy, peppy and optimistic. At that point I didn't know what torture was to come. The doctor weighed me and asked me to come in again in a few weeks for my next prenatal check-up.

At the next appointment, I heard something I wasn't expecting at all.

"What have you been doing??" the doctor asked, as she weighed me. "How did you gain weight so quickly?"

"I've been eating bread. A lot of it."

Apparently a bread-based diet was something my body didn't particularly like. Or, maybe it liked it a bit too much.

It was hard for me to receive a scolding for the quick weight gain, but I understood her concern over bulking up on empty bread calories instead of nutrient-rich food. But try as I did to be mindful of eating healthy, nausea and acid reflux did not help.

In addition to seeing my family doctor, I was referred to an OB/GYN. Very early on I told the nurses (who checked my weight upon arrival) to not tell me what my weight was. I asked them to tell me only if there was anything alarming (not gaining, or gaining too much). Otherwise, I didn't think I could handle watching the numbers climb each week. I don't recall telling them my history and explaining why this was, but they likely figured it out. I resolved to simply eat what I could eat, and hoped my body would respond by doing what it needed to do. And that's what I did.

I'm not sure what my final weight was at the end of that pregnancy. I remember being very uncomfortable in my own skin. I felt huge carrying the baby and the added weight around. I knew my body needed the extra fat, increased blood and fluid to sustain the baby and for breastfeeding afterwards, so I tried my best to make peace with it. Even though I knew this, it was still damn hard. My breasts were big- I hated that. I'm not sure how huge my ass was- but I hated that too. Maternity clothes were lacking in style then, so I felt hideous and frumpy. We didn't have a local maternity store at the time so being fashion forward was pretty much impossible. Finding a maternity bathing suit was an absolute nightmare.

At the time, someone in our circle (a male) made a comment that I believe was meant to be "positive", but that I didn't perceive as such. He said that I was "one of those girls who would bounce back after having the baby."

That callous statement doesn't acknowledge the changes that a woman goes through to have a child. They are significant changes that we don't just "bounce back" from. Many things don't "go back" at all. Part of me knew this was a ridiculous and unrealistic expectation. But another part of me didn't process this well. It made me feel as though my worth was attached to my looks, or to what others thought of me. It made me feel like a failure if I couldn't make this happen. It made me feel that I had to get my pre-pregnancy body back so that my husband would still find me attractive and worthy. Luckily he didn't make me feel this way. However, I have known men who put such pressures on their partners.

I'd like to punch them all in the face.

MY DAYS AS A DAIRY COW

So, I went and did it. I created a little human being and evacuated it successfully from my body. The instant 10 lb weight loss felt pretty good, but then I had to deal with the rest of the post-pregnancy stuff.

The nurse came into my room on several occasions and massaged my belly, to help my uterus contract. Although I had taken the prenatal classes and read all go-to books on being pregnant and having a baby, I wasn't expecting what happened. It was like a (bloodless) scene from a strange horror movie- her hand disappeared into an abyss of stretched-out excessive skin, fat, and a hollow uterus. It looked nothing like my youthful pre-children belly.

I was clearly not prepared for the physical changes. I guess as much as you try, you can't totally prep for such a thing. Being young and inexperienced, I was still quite modest after having my first baby. While in active labour, I didn't bat an eye about who was all-up in my hoo-ha. If I thought someone could stop the pain and/or get the baby out, they had been welcome.

Post-delivery was a different story though. The delivery had not gone smoothly, and I had almost needed an emergency c-section. Afterwards, I was still hooked up to an IV and in rough shape. As a result, I needed assistance going to the bathroom. My younger self could never have predicted that I'd ever have another person in the bathroom with me, changing my very bloody pad. She had probably done this sort of thing thousands of times, but it was my first. I was embarrassed. I asked her if she had any children of her own, to which she replied that she had one. That made me feel a bit better, knowing we had shared the same awful experience of filling a huge pad diaper with big disgusting blood clots.

Childbirth is such a beautiful, natural thing.

Another "natural" thing (that being breastfeeding) was also a disaster my first time around. My newborn son was not able to latch. At that time, we didn't know that he had been born with a significant genetic condition, which was why he was unable to latch like a newborn typically could.

"I've never seen anything like this, even with preemies," the lactation expert shared. "Usually the premature babies can still be taught how to nurse. It's almost like he has a backwards suck."

Unfortunately, not knowing at this time that he had a disability, I blamed myself for failing at breastfeeding. It was traumatic for me. I couldn't even nourish my baby. I had already failed as a mother.

Although my son couldn't nurse, I pumped (and we fed him by bottle), so my milk came in quite fast. And when I say it came in, boy did it come in. One of my nurses, upon entering my hospital room, lit up and exclaimed "woah! Your milk came in!"

And yes it had. Not only did my milk come in, I think the whole milk truck came in. I could have breastfed the entire floor of babies. Those puppies blew up to the size of my head.

Because I was a new mother, the nurses offered me a lot of guidance. They each tried in their own way to get him to latch. This meant I had to get over any modesty with my breasts pretty quick. My breasts have never gotten so much handling ever, and likely never will again.

On one occasion, a nurse gave into the frustration and tried a different strategy. She scolded him, my breast in her hand, waving it as well as you can wave a big engorged breast, trying to get the nipple in his mouth and a proper latch. It didn't work, but it was a moment I will never forget. Sadly comical, it was. I was incredibly grateful for the multitude of help the nurses gave, even if it was a bust.

A bust.

I continued to pump so I could give him breast milk by bottle. It was a choice I'm glad I made, but it was hard. I missed out on a process that I felt was natural, and the bonding that went with it. I was exhausted from the extra time that was needed to pump and feed him by bottle. He was slow to feed from the bottle, which was tiring. He didn't sleep well, which meant that I in turn did not sleep well. I ended up with infections in both breasts from erratic pumping, and became quite sick as a result.

I pumped for 6 weeks. Sometimes I wonder how long I would have continued on that path had I not been told to stop. After a continuing medical complication, the doctor instructed me to stop pumping and give him only formula. Following the doctor's orders was a blessing- it gave me permission to stop and let go of the guilt I had in doing so. The change to only formula did help the issue significantly, so it was the right choice.

* * *

Two years later... I delivered my 2nd child, a girl. My pregnancy with her had been pretty terrible too. But the labour was very fast, the delivery much smoother. I felt such a rush and was energetic afterward. The 10lb instant weight loss again was fantastic. I was able to get myself to the bathroom and change my own pad! I felt great, a little too great. On the day I delivered her, I was up walking around, making trips to the kitchen to get juice and other things. My milk had come in quickly, and my breasts were so enormous that no remaining belly was visible. It didn't look like I had just had a baby. A breast enhancement, yes. A baby, no.

That day, my doctor saw me in the hall. "I didn't realize that was you," he said. "You need to go lay down and rest. You're going to regret being so active if you don't."

Boy, was that doctor right.

Breastfeeding baby #2 was a success, although I had a lot of problems with pain in the beginning. After a few weeks the pain subsided; it later went away altogether. Even while it was painful, I was determined to stick it out because I had been so regretful about not being able to nurse my first. And perhaps that made me even more stubborn, because I made the decision to solely nurse her, and not give her any formula. In hindsight, this was not the best idea for me- she also refused to take a bottle of breast milk, thus relying on me as her only food source.

I was a busy and tired mama with a newborn and a 2 year old (with a disability). Some of my best multi-tasking took place during the act of breastfeeding my daughter. I also taught her how to nurse laying down, so I could take advantage of the down time and rest. At night I was often up with my son, so I was fairly sleep-deprived. I couldn't afford any more sleep deprivation. When the wee one would wake through the night for a feeding, I'd retrieve her from her crib, lay her down beside me and she'd go ahead and help herself. Out of curiosity, mothers often ask each other how many times babies wake up through the night to feed. I usually had no idea. My response was typically "I'm not sure. I lay her down with me, and it's self-serve."

I nursed baby #2 for a full year, so I did get used to feeding her in public. As anyone who has breastfed a baby (and her partner and her other children) likely know... breastfeeding happens so frequently that the breast becomes completely non-sexual. You get accustomed to whipping out a breast when needed, wherever needed.

The one thing I had a hard time adjusting to was the amount of milk that I produced. I seemed to make a lot. I feared feeding her at a restaurant and having her break the latch mid-feed, putting the customers at the next table at risk of being sprayed.

I would have made an incredible dairy cow.

While producing milk easily is a blessing when feeding your

baby, it's not fun to spend so much of your day leaking. I had to go shopping for bras and a bathing suit when I was a new mom, which was not an ideal time. If you're a woman, you should be familiar with the rule about keeping on your own underwear while you try on new underwear or a bathing suit. I have yet to meet the underwear police (or whoever enforces this), but there is the assumption that you will not break this rule. Therefore, when you buy a bathing suit, you can feel assured that 52 women did not have their moist crotch touching your suit... provided they all complied.

I am assuming that there is a special kind of hell for women who have not been baptized AND broke the underwear rule.

Well, when you're leaking milk non-stop from your ta-tas it is very difficult to keep your dairy off the bra or bathing suit you're trying on, even if you are well intentioned. I felt rather guilty leaking all over the clothing. But at least I kept my undies on.

❈ ❈ ❈

Fast forward four more years... we welcomed baby #3. Like her sister, I also breastfed her for nearly a full year.

I'm very happy that I breastfed my children, but I was definitely done by the end. I appreciated having my body back. One cute memory from that time is remembering how their faces would light up when they'd see me change- because they could see boobs, their comforting food source. Babies don't judge- they just think breasts are beautiful and yummy.

❈ ❈ ❈

Only a few weeks after I had delivered our third child, their father and I took our kids to an indoor amusement park for our son's birthday. I struggled getting ready to leave the house. I was in that in between stage of not wanting to wear maternity clothes, but other clothes didn't fit. I felt frumpy and overweight. I found something to put on and sucked it up so we could go have a good time with the kids.

The park was relatively empty that day, because most children were still in school. We pretty much had free run of the entire place. We walked from ride to ride, getting on whatever we liked. We played a lot of the games with our little guy, but we also went on some of the low rides, like the kids' train.

And there was the carousel. The sweet carousel, with its playful music, loved by every child and adult. The horses that go up and down... up and down... I'm not a fan of heights, so riding the carousel with the 2 older children was a seemingly perfect idea. Our newborn baby stayed on the side with her father.

A minute or so into the ride, we heard some clunking and dragging and it became apparent that there was something terribly wrong with the ride. I thought the metal canopy was going to collapse on our heads. The ride jammed to a stop, lopsided. I managed to rescue both of the kids and get them to safety, then I collapsed onto a nearby bench and sobbed, scared and embarrassed. The staff were extremely apologetic and gave us free passes to come another time (why would I want to do that???) I continued sobbing. I didn't go on any more rides, but their dad did some activities with the older children. I sat with the baby, nursed her, and sobbed some more.

I was mortified. I was so heavy that I had broken the carousel.

❈ ❈ ❈

I somehow managed to survive the process of pregnancy and childbirth THREE times (and all of my pregnancies were terrible). There is something remarkable about the maternal instinct, and how it helps us to forget the pain that comes with childbirth.

That's my nice way of saying that hormones make you forgetful and dumb.

DEFLATED

According to Google's dictionary, deflated means "having suddenly lost confidence or optimism."
Ladies who have breastfed, you know what I'm talking about- I've lost confidence and optimism in my breasts. Yes, after three children, my breasts became deflated.

As a young woman, I had been told of the importance of doing regular breast self-exams by health care providers.

Put your arm up, hold your fingers like so, do this motion, go over the breast like this, don't miss anywhere. Make sure to feel into the armpit as well. Note any lumps or irregularities. Repeat on the other side. Make sure to do this every month. Don't forget- your breasts will change throughout your cycle, and also with age and hormonal changes.

WHAT??!?!?

I haven't felt a lot of breasts in my day, so I'm not sure what the average 20 year old's breast feels like. I'm just going on my own limited experience here...but my breasts were lumpy, chunky, bumpy, dense bastards. I would not have been capable of finding a suspicious lump in my breast. The thought of being able to find one was astonishing to me.

In university, I had a roommate whose mother had fought breast cancer for many years, and eventually lost that fight. At only 20 years old, my roommate was an advocate for promoting self-breast exams. I knew the seriousness of doing so, but I still struggled to understand how I'd be able to detect anything without professional assistance.

However, a funny thing happened after pumping and breastfeeding babies- all those lumpy bumpies in there disappeared. *Where the heck did they go??? Did the babies suck out small masses of breast tissue or whatever was in there?*

My lactating breasts had been the size of small planets, and so when the milk dried up they were left rather stretched out. To be honest, I've experienced brief moments when I've wished I had not breastfed, but they've passed rather quickly. Whenever the thoughts of perky boobs trigger pangs of longing, I remind myself of the times I bonded with and nourished my children. I also remind myself that I am no longer in my 20s, and my body is how it is supposed to be.

Surprisingly, I only got light stretch marks on my small planets, and they faded. It was so minimal that it didn't really bother me. And I lucked out in terms of stretch marks on my belly, because despite the substantial pregnancy weight gains I didn't get stretch marks there. I actually had quite a flat stomach after my first two children. I wasn't a buffed-out gymnast by any means, but it was a surprise to many that I had carried two babies to term.

And then there was pregnancy #3.

I adore my third child. So, I say this with great love when I speak ill of my excess belly skin. Yup. I ended up with the mom apron. And love handles. Whatever else all that lovely extra skin and bit of fat is called. The problem with that extra skin is that it never disappears. If you lose weight, it just hangs looser, which isn't such a great look. The only option is to have it surgically removed. Don't get me wrong- it's crossed my mind. And unlike surgically changing one's nose, surgically removing my belly flab wouldn't change my look and make me unrecognizable to my children, right?

Of course, not a lot of mothers of three can afford to pay for this kind of elective surgery. And I was one of them.

I've often thought about this pooch. *If I had the opportunity to remove the extra skin, would I?* I've been strongly determined to set a good example for my daughters, which includes accepting one's body as it is. Even if that body or parts of it seem "imperfect." *What message would I be giving them if I opted for a surgical modification?*

Part of me will always wonder…if the cost of the procedure were not a deterrent…would I have had the surgery? I like to think that I wouldn't. Then again, if I were to have it done at this point in my life for me, that's a personal choice and there should be nothing wrong with that. Truth be told, I have such issues with my abdomen and things fitting around the waist (which causes pain) that I think there would be real benefits to me not having the excessive roll of flesh there.

There are such ridiculous expectations for women to look a certain way to be considered attractive, sexy, or "healthy." But… I created a baby. A human life. It grew inside of me. I supported that little being from within my own body for a whole 9 months. And then continued to feed it after as well. And I did it THREE times. I need to cut myself a little slack for the stretching and sagging I endured as a result.

I think sometimes as women we are so focused on our own bodies and how they've changed from our youth, that we forget to notice that our men change as well, and that's ok. We should not be expected to stay looking like we did when we were 20. None of us.

That's what I keep telling myself anyway. I'm pretty sure I'm right, but I have to keep reminding myself of it.

THINGS MAY NOT BE AS THEY SEEM

Many years ago I read an article about women's tendency to adopt a distorted sense of self, and our inability to often to see ourselves as the size we really are. Simple experiments have been executed to support this. Basically, it involves showing a row of female silhouette figures, aligned from smallest to largest (or a variation of this). The participant is then asked to choose the silhouette that best represents her own size. Findings show that a large percentage of women cannot guess the body that comes closest to representing their own size. But what was more interesting was that women who didn't guess correctly tended to choose a *larger* figure than their size, instead of a smaller one. From this we could deduce that most women think they are bigger than they really are.

In a way it doesn't surprise me that people would choose wrong, because we can't objectively SEE ourselves, in person anyway. However, the fact that so many women assume themselves as larger than they are says something about our weight culture.

I would fail that test miserably. I'm so lousy at judging my size that I often take 3 different sized (same) garments into a changing room to try on. I was also always unable to judge my facial attractiveness. I didn't know I was attractive. Even when I did eventually get attention from males (more so in university than high school), I still didn't really *know* it.

Once, a very long time ago, a friend made a comment out of the blue about me being too thin.

"WHAT??!?? What are you talking about?? Have you looked in a mirror?" I fired back.

Yes, this friend was slim and tiny, with a very pleasing figure. Yet, when I tried to tell her that I was bigger than her, she kept insisting that I was not. It agitated me, so I didn't let it go. Somehow I felt like there was judgement in her statement, which rattled me. *Why was she making a judgement about my size? Especially when she was slim herself?*

I'm not sure why we settled on thighs as a comparison point, but we did. There we were- trying to determine who had the bigger thighs. Eventually I retrieved a measuring tape (I was not losing this battle!) and we measured with accuracy the size of the widest point of our thighs.

They measured the exact same. I was clearly not the only person who did not have an accurate picture of myself.

I'm still not sure where her sudden statement had come from. Even though we are considerably separated now by distance, I still consider her to be a friend. She was an invaluable support to me through my divorce. Some things are much more important than the size of one's thighs.

❋ ❋ ❋

I was out with (female) friends many years ago when I was newly separated, a rare event at the time. I was the only single woman of the few that were there. We were talking about dating and being younger and hooking up. One of my friends (who has had challenges with her weight) talked about how she loves sex, and in her younger days she loved having casual sex without any commitment. I was quite shocked to hear this. She is very sweet and always seemed to be a bit shy, so it wasn't something I expected to hear. Then she talked about how she was a bit smaller in size (never tiny) but she had so much confidence then and felt very sexy.

I felt a bit envious when she revealed this. I had never had this kind of confidence, ever. In my surprise, I said "really?? I wish I could be that confident."

It was her time to look shocked. She blurted out something like "if I looked like you, I'd be out hooking up all the time!"

The truth is, I didn't see that. Not when I was young before kids, not after kids. Yes, there were times when I would get dressed up, put on makeup, do my hair and feel pretty. But I didn't feel consistently pretty. I felt like I always needed a lot of help to be pretty. If I didn't have makeup on, it was painful to look someone in the eye if I ran into them at the grocery store. I'm not sure where that insecurity came from. I felt a bit like an ugly duckling when I was an underdeveloped teenager, and by the time I flourished I still couldn't see it; I still identified as that ugly duckling, I guess.

HAIR ENVY LED TO DISASTER

When I was very young, my parents made the decision to grow my hair very long. Or maybe they made the decision to not cut it. Or maybe they forgot to make a decision, hence why it just kept growing. Whatever the case, it was freakin' long.

Long hair seemed to be the standard then for girls- girls had long hair, boys had short hair, and anything other than that was questionable or straight-out wrong. Even in the teen years, it was (and I believe may still be) perceived that males who grow their hair long are usually trying to make a statement- bad boy, rebel, carefree... whatever the case, long hair on a teenage boy or grown man is not the norm and can be considered in many circles to be unprofessional.

Back to my youthful hair woes...

My hair was very long, very straight and very blonde. Even at a young age, one often longs for what they can't have. My best friend had long hair. It was a beautiful brown, and she had curls. Curls. Oh how I was in love with those sweet, loose curls. I still recall how genuinely sad I was when she cut her hair in elementary school and many of those curls were subsequently lost. I was even more sad in high school when she purposefully straightened her hair. It seemed entirely wrong to deny the world those beautiful soft curls.

Yes, I had hair envy, even from a very young age.

Like everything else with my body, I didn't appreciate my hair. If I look back and consider it, it was a very pretty shade of blonde, natural highlights and lowlights throughout. You know, the stuff that women pay big bucks for now at a salon. It was very fine and very healthy. It was easy to manage in the sense that it was low maintenance. But oh, how I wanted to change my hair.

I was discouraged from cutting my hair at an early age. Of course, I didn't have the money for a haircut or the means to get to a hairdresser, so I was pretty much stuck with it as is. At one point it reached my bum.

My mother used to do the trim because it was pretty easy to do, which seemed to be the norm for many children that age at that time- we got the "mom haircut." I guess I should be lucky she didn't do a bowl cut, or a sexy 80's mullet.

I always got excited for hair trimming day. I would be asked to sit on a chair in the kitchen, very still. I learned a "trick" which I often employed to try to get more hair cut than she intended. If I tipped my head backwards slightly, the top layer of my hair would sit more forward. After she cut it all even I would straighten my head back up. As a result, the layer underneath became exposed. My poor mother would become frustrated because despite her best efforts it wouldn't be even. She would then have to cut more off, as I quietly contained my excitement about my accomplishment. If I was lucky I could get an extra inch cut off. Had my mother been one to curse, I'm sure I would have learned some colourful new words.

I was a very honest child, so this was as deceptive as I got (except for pocketing those disgusting greasy sausages, aka Satan's fingers).

When I got to university, it was a time for me to step out of my shell (as well as self-destruct, as previously detailed). Changing my hair seemed like the obvious means to change the way I looked, the way I felt, and the way I presented myself to the world.

I wasn't entirely wrong to think this way. A hair change can definitely affect the way you think about yourself. Just think about those makeover shows where people get new wardrobes and makeup... changing/updating their hair is a big part of their transformation.

With great hesitation, I will share a few of my hair transformations...

* * *

Hair Disaster #1
Goal: Thicker Hair
When I was around 18, my hair was so fine (and healthy) that it would slip out of any type of hairstyle I fruitlessly tried to give myself. I felt it had no depth or interest. I eventually mustered enough courage to cut my hair to about shoulder length, but no further. Despite this huge act of brevity, my hair still fell lifeless, just shorter. I went to countless hairstylists to ask their professional opinion about my hair. I was convinced one would have a technique or strategy for getting some dimension and thickness into my hair. Much to my dismay, their responses also kept falling flat. They told me that I was out of luck and that I was destined to have uneventful hair. I kept desperately searching, never sticking with the same stylist because I was hoping that one would finally figure out how to get me some thickness. It turns out, the only thing that was thick was my skull.

End result: Disappointment and mid-length, flat, lifeless hair.

Lesson learned: You can lead a horse to water, but you can't make its hair any thicker.

* * *

Hair Disaster #2
Goal: Get Some Curl
As we all now know, I had some serious curl envy. Not only

did I love the look of curls and waves, but I thought that a bit of wave would give my hair some body. Because my hair lacked any sort of natural body, I decided to try something that would help give me that body- a perm.

I know, I know. Keep in mind, this was the 1990's. It seemed like a good idea at the time (like other bad 90's trends). I'm not sure what I was expecting, but my closest experience with perms until this point had been from the girl who sat in front of me in high school, her long perfect spiralling curls cascading onto my desk. They were beautiful and even held the pleasing scent of her shampoo. I loved them.

I was going to have those curls.

I remember Perm Day very clearly. I went to a salon near campus at the mall. I explained to the woman that I wanted a perm, but my hair didn't hold curl well. In my defence, she validated this, testing my hair to see how it held a curl. Seeing that it didn't hold well, we decided to go with a smaller, tighter spiral. I sat through the process with anticipation, with both positive excitement and dreadful nervousness.

The end result was tragic. I looked like a poodle. My taste in dog breeds has expanded since then, but at that time I did not like poodles. And I was one. I somehow managed to shove all my tears down deep inside my abdomen, for fear of hurting the hairstylist's feelings. I suspect she knew that I was distraught, but I still tried to spare her from my true angst.

The smell of the chemicals in my hair was a repulsive reminder of what I had done to myself.

UGH.

As soon as I left the mall, I pulled my hair back into a ponytail as best I could. I was mortified, and didn't want anyone to see what I had done to my hair. I went back to residence, and quickly went to the shower with a bottle of shampoo, where I spent an hour repeatedly washing my hair. I was trying to get the chemicals to relax as best as they could. While this helped, the desperate excessive washing still couldn't restore it to its natural state. Luckily my roommate had many years of hair straightening experience, so she helped me through this time. And counselled me. I kept my hair pulled back for months, and very few people even realized what I had done. If they had, they certainly hadn't dared to tell me.

End result: Damaged frizzy hair and psychological trauma.

Lesson learned: You can lead a horse to the salon, but it might end up leaving as a poodle.

※ ※ ※

Hair Disaster #3

Goal: Even-Out the Color

By the time this hair disaster happened, I was accustomed to my hair plans not working out as intended. Therefore, I exercised added caution, thinking it was enough to keep me out of deep trouble. I was wrong.

The summer sun had bleached out my hair quite a bit. Not wanting to be left with the big, bold roots of new growth coming in, I had a plan to tone down the lighter hair to better blend-in with the new growth. Buying a hair dye kit that matched the blonde seemed relatively easy, and much more inexpensive than going to a salon. As a student trying to live on limited funds, this seemed like the logical thing to do.

I went to the drug store with my friend and got her help in matching my hair to the (fake) hair samples that were paired with the hair dye boxes. My hair always had a multitude of shades naturally in it, which made finding a solid shade a bit of a challenge, but we did find one that closely matched my untouched protected darker blonde underneath. I was satisfied with and confident in my choice.

I performed the operation at the university residence. Again, I should have had mental health professionals on standby. The end result did NOT look like that fake hair sample. It did NOT look like the box. It was very, very, very bad.

Synonyms for "bad" (compliments of Thesaurus.com):

atrocious, awful, crummy, dreadful, lousy, poor, sad, unacceptable, blah, bummer, downer, garbage, gross, imperfect, inferior, junky, synthetic, abominable, amiss, beastly, cruddy, crappy, defective, deficient, dissatisfactory, faulty, god-awful, icky, inadequate, the pits, substandard...

...and, my personal favourite... not good.

It was all of those things. Very *not good*.

What happened is that the hair that had been most exposed to the sun and had been bleached blonder than the rest picked up an *icky* ashy grey tone from the hair dye. Now, an ashy grey tone might have been the "in" thing around 2018, but it was not in the 90's. Also, the undamaged hair (the hair that had been protected underneath, as well as the new growth at the roots) took on a *synthetic* reddish pigment.

I had *god-awful* grey and red hair.

Of course, I was devastated by this *gross* and *crummy* development. And my attempt to save money turned into anything but. I went to a salon, cried, and begged for help. While I was there the stylists decided to tell me that my hair was not really ashy grey, but more of an *abominable* green. I cried harder. It was not a very helpful clarification, thank you stylists.

The professionals tried to correct my *unacceptable, sad* hair. They stripped the color out, and put color back in. But to their bewilderment, my *deficient* hair kept taking the color incorrectly. After several *dissatisfactory* attempts, they gave up. So, not only did I have hideous *defective* hair, but also a big bill to pay.

I then did what any desperate gal would do - I went to another salon. They also tried to get my hair to take color properly, but it would not. They tried as best they could, then told me they couldn't do any more as they were worried that my *faulty* hair would literally break and I'd have no hair. I begged them to leave it stripped of color (which was a bleached-out look) but they said they couldn't. They even tried to deposit color that would render me a redhead, but it still would not take the color uniformly. I ended up leaving the salon with *crappy* red and green hair, and was even more poor and *imperfect.*

Those next few weeks were some of the lowest ones in my life. I was at the height of my depression anyway, and now I looked like a freak. It was hard for me to go to class. I tried to find ways to wear my hair so that it was less noticeable, but was not successful. In the end, I wore a baseball cap- the cap covered my reddish roots and where it met the *lousy* grey/green hair. The length of my hair then went out through the hole of the baseball cap, which I then wove into a long braid. The *blah* braid seemed to help blend the colors a little, so it was a little less *dreadful.*

Luckily the color faded out as time went on, making the obvious less obvious. I eventually was able to stop wearing a hat, and resumed my life outside of my dorm room and classroom.

End result: a braided "Ann of Green Gables" look, with green hair interspersed.

Lesson learned: Horses look stupid with red and green/grey hair.

* * *

Around 13 years ago when my youngest was wee, I cut my hair quite significantly. It was actually shorter than the haircut I had tried in university during my self-reinventing phase. While I received quite a number of compliments on my chin-length hair, *it didn't feel like me.* As much as I tried, I could not identify with shorter hair.

Although I had always wanted to have a trendy hairstyle, I started to realize it wouldn't suit me. I once worked with a young woman who changed her hair all the time. One month it would be a certain color, the next it would be entirely different. Or she would have a different cut. I asked her one day what her boyfriend thought of it (usually if I contemplated changing my hair, I was met with resistance from males). Her response "he really likes it. It's like being with a different woman all the time." Smart guy. Might as well have fun with it. I just hope he was able to remember her name.

Since then, I have made leaps and bounds reconciling my hair issues. I eventually decided that I like my hair. Sure, I'd make it a bit thicker if it could be, but I'm quite happy with it as is. I've learned to use products that make my hair a bit less slippery so it will stay up better if I try to secure it back. I finally appreciate how low maintenance it is. I love being able to pull it back easily out of my face into a ponytail or a reckless messy bun. My hair has darkened as I've aged but because I like the blonde, I get highlights from time to time- not so much that I need to go to the salon often. My hairstylist has mastered hair color that suits me (no more green or red!), and she's hilarious to boot, so I enjoy our time together of laughing and catching up. I also came to the conclusion that my hair is one of my best physical attributes, so I appreciate rather than reject it.

I'm not sure what the future will bring if (when) my hair thins or I lose it. But, you know what? I will deal with that if and when it happens, and won't worry about it in the meantime. That's something my 20 year old self could not have said.

※ ※ ※

I wonder when long hair (historically speaking) became equated with femininity. I would suspect this differs between cultural groups, as different types (and texture) of hair are managed in different ways. It would be interesting to study though- *what was the reasoning behind this? Why was there a general distinction?*

I suspect as gender becomes less binary and divided that these ideals of (femininity) and (masculinity) will fade. I tried to raise my daughters to be willing to express themselves how they like, and tried not to put pressure on them to keep their hair long, although it's been hard. (I was socialized to like long hair on girls, and I honestly do prefer it.) I must have succeeded because as soon as my daughter turned 14, she chopped her hair off and dyed a blue streak in it. I was (am) proud of her for doing what she wanted to do. Instead of it being an act of rebellion, it was just a personal decision of style.

I know my partner loves my hair as it is. He would likely feel a little sad if I told him I intended to cut it off. At the same time, he would never tell me not to. And he would love me just as much with no hair or blue hair. It's true, hairstyle can play into an initial attraction with someone, but if you really like who a person is, their hairstyle becomes pretty insignificant, or it should. As I've gotten older, I have learned to appreciate these decisions that I make about my body, or other parts of my life, decisions that I don't make based on anyone else's beliefs. Decisions I make for ME.

Women aren't the only ones who struggle with hair identity in their 40's. I've known many men who are self-conscious and feel cruddy about balding. Sure, there's plenty of teasing around a man losing his hair. But, like other times that people poke fun of themselves, the jokes are often to hide their feelings of insecurity and loss.

Again, humour as a coping skill. I'm far from the only one who uses this.

I've spoken with men who dappled with longer locks in their past. They wistfully talk about their younger years when they had long hair… Their eyes do this thing where they glaze over… their souls detach from their body…they transport back to that time…

I'm convinced that every guy who had long hair in his teens or young 20's thinks he was super incredibly hot with that long hair. When they show me a photo, I usually have to stifle a laugh.

Guys…you looked just as hot as I looked at that age with my teased bangs. It's beastly. Let it go.

MID-LIFE DATING AND THE PERFECT COOKIE

I wasn't a fan of dating in my teens to early 20's. In fact, I had successfully avoided it for the most part. Haven gotten married at 24, I thought I had sealed my romantic fate and would never again have to try to navigate those muddy waters. When I found myself with 3 children, separated and out in the dating world again at 35, I was not thrilled.

By that age, I had acquired more wisdom. As such, I had (naively) thought that I would be more at ease with dating and meeting people this time around. Of course, my role models (if you could call them that) were fictional female characters on TV who were in the dating world. They had aged with grace. They were sassy and exuded an attractive confidence. They knew their worth. They may not have had the youthful beauty of a 20 year old, but they didn't need it. That was going to be me. I wouldn't have any major issues meeting men and with the dating process, because of all my personal growth over the years.

INSERT LAUGH HERE.

What I found was, I was still terrified to have a new person in my personal space. I was still nervous in conversation. I still second-guessed myself. I was confused by my feelings- *did I like him? Did he like me?* I felt like I was 17 again trying to figure it all out. And as much as the prospect of a new love interest can be kind of exciting, it was not enough to make me enjoy the process.

However at this point in my life, it wasn't just me I was considering. This person was also going to be in the lives of my three young children. This added a lot more pressure. And to make things even more complicated, men in their 30's usually come with children of their own. That makes even more potential for conflict with personalities and general logistics; blending families can be very difficult.

Single, young, non-parents with less "history" have it much easier when it comes to dating. But, it's one of those things you don't realize at the time, until you look back and realize how easy you really had it.

In regards to insecurities with my looks... by this point I had somewhat clued in that I was considered to be attractive and had aged well, but... I still didn't really *know* it. I can't see myself. I can't experience myself from another perspective, and each perspective is different. Beauty and attractiveness are subjective.

Over the years, men have questioned me on my inability to see my physical attractiveness. The question "do you not realize how beautiful you are?" was one I had been asked a few times.

No, no I don't. *Am I really? Like, now? Still? Is my figure pleasing too?*

I believe everyone is beautiful in their own way, just as I believe people are smart in their own way. I just wish I had felt it a bit more myself; perhaps dating would not have been so painful.

I knew I didn't want to rely on physical attractiveness to find a partner anyway. I wanted to be found attractive primarily for my quirkiness and personality. I was hoping that I was physically attractive enough for that to be a bonus.

Luckily I had learned to adopt an if-he-doesn't-like-it-then-it's-his-problem-and-he-doesn't-deserve-it attitude. But, the funny thing is, I didn't get any complaints anyway.

✳ ✳ ✳

In my younger days, I frequented bars. I had spent a number of years going out with friends, for the main purpose of dancing. I did enjoy some attention from young men there, but that's as far as it went. I was a very tame person, so hooking up with people was not my thing.

By the time I started dating again in my 30's, I was well out of the bar scene, so meeting people at a club or pub wasn't an option. I had also reasoned that it wasn't the ideal location to find a partner anyway; if someone were a parent, I would hope that they were parenting and not out at the bars, myself included. Finding eligible single men was therefore a bit of a challenge. I had no luck finding any through my employment situation, so I turned to where many my age nowadays look to find a potential suitor: an online dating website.

It wasn't very long ago that online dating sites didn't even exist. And it wasn't that long ago that online dating sites were thought to be only used by lonely gamers who never left their houses. I had been friends with a young woman in university some 15 years prior who met a man this way (gaming). She moved out of the country to marry him. Everyone thought she was crazy. We lost touch, but I like to think she's still happily married, gaming with her true love from opposite ends of their home while eating Doritos.

Nowadays it's not considered to be completely shameful or a declaration of your loser status if you meet someone online. However, if you try to explain to someone from an older generation how you met someone from a dating website... be prepared for some strange looks and doubtful questions and comments. Hey, I'm a busy, picky person- I'm not going to partner up with Joe across the street just because he's an available male in my age bracket. And my parents have yet to arrange any marriage for me, so I've had to resort to using the web as a screening tool for a mate.

I had actually met a number of very nice, respectable people through the dating site. Yes, very nice non-psychopath men who aren't just interested in one-night stands do look for potential partners online.

I had been hesitant to make my dating profile public, especially my photo. Exposing who I was and attaching my real picture to it made me feel very vulnerable. I was worried my ex would see it, my brother would see it, my friends would see it, my cat would see it, people from my community would see it. Then I thought- *why do I care so much? They're only seeing it if they're on there too. In that case, they're equally as loserish as me.* In theory, if I'm telling the truth about who I am, I shouldn't worry about who sees it and who reads it.

The first time I had tried online dating, I didn't make my pictures visible. Well, when I drug my feet back to the website again the last time (at almost 42), I decided I was going to fully commit to the process and allow my photo to be seen. For the most part, it was a positive experience. One thing that really helped me is having had a good friend share with me valuable lessons she had learned from her past online dating adventures. One of such lessons was: if you are going to include a photo, it needs to be a headshot. Nothing below the shoulders.

Men are visual creatures. They can get distracted from meaningful conversations when you introduce breasts too quickly into the equation. My friend (who usually tried to play down her well-endowed breasts) had man upon man upon man make comments about her chest. It got to the point that she weeded out potential suitors based on this- if they commented about her breasts in the first few exchanges she didn't continue to chat with them.

In order to help keep out any temptations to initiate crude talk, all of the photos I shared were shoulders and up. No boobs. No ass. Not even a foot. And a great thing happened- men didn't focus on or ever comment about my body, because they hadn't seen it to comment on.

I learned right away that online dating photos could be very deceiving. Of course, users want to post favourable photos of themselves, to pique interest in others. But sometimes they'd use photos that didn't offer a true representation, whether they were trying to be deceptive or not. They may have noticeably aged or gained or lost weight since the photo was taken.

And then became the big issue of camera and photo filters. Unfortunately there are no filters in real life to make us look that smooth and refreshed. At that time, I spoke with several men who shared very interesting stories about meeting a woman for the first time. Between filters, photos from younger days and huge amounts of makeup, they weren't quite sure whom they were meeting.

I try to subscribe to the looks-shouldn't-matter-it's-the-personality-that-should-count thing, but let's face it, they do. I didn't want to meet someone and see the look of disappointment on his face if I didn't look like my pictures. So, I posted photos that were not high-end, and had no filters. That's not to say that I looked terrible (no, I didn't spring a pajamas and no makeup kinda picture on them), but I didn't give false expectations. And the few people that I met told me that I looked like my pictures, which they were pleased about.

Clearly I had mastered Pictures for Online Dating 101.

Let's be honest, if I were to use filters, I'd be taking photos of my ass, not my face. And then I'd post that perfect ass photo all over social media. I'd make sure to label it and tag myself in it, so everyone knew it was my ass...

In addition to the photos I shared, there was the consideration of how would I present myself in my profile description. I found that part to be somewhat easy. My profile description wasn't so much about the kind of person I wanted to be with, but more about who I was, and what was important to me. I put a lot of thought into it because I wanted to attract the right kind of person. As a result, I got a ton of positive feedback about my profile. I received compliments from people who told me straight out that they weren't a good match for me, but that they just wanted to tell me how impressed they were by the work put into the description. If you've spent any time on those sites, you've probably seen that a great number of profiles are just thrown on without much thought. Or they'll post a list of qualities that they want in someone. Like they're shopping for ingredients to make their favourite cookies.

- ✓ flour
- ✓ butter
- ✓ salt
- ✓ oats
- ✓ chocolate chips

I've never understood how people make a list and think that they'll find a match based on that list. A connection is so much more than a list of qualities. And, all "chocolate chips" are not created equal. *Do you prefer the punch of a semi-sweet chip, or would you rather play it safe with milk chocolate?*

For me, there's a major drawback to online dating: I can't tell if I like someone (physically) by a photo alone. It's like... I see the picture of the cookie. The cookie looks pretty good. It looks like it baked up perfectly. But I can't taste the cookie through the photo.

A picture is flat. When it comes to attraction, I'm drawn to mannerisms, the cute way someone talks, the way they wrinkle their nose, the awkward smiles... those things are not captured in a photo. Therefore, it meant I had to actually meet people, which... ugh. I didn't like meeting people because I didn't want to give them a false expectation or let them down when I didn't see that nose wrinkle or little crooked grin that I'd think was adorable.

If you go through the effort of ordering the cookie, the cookie is going to be disappointed if you don't at least try it. I hate disappointing cookies.

But... if I didn't take the chance to check out the other parts of the bakery, I'd risk getting stuck with a cookie flavour that wasn't really my favourite. There's not enough milk in the world to choke those down for the rest of your life.

I learned that I am far from the only person with body hang-ups at this age. Online dating allows you to screen out people who are under a certain height, over a certain height, over or under a certain size, and over or under a certain age. You just enter in all your criteria and POOF!! the perfect person shows up gift wrapped at your door.

Ok, maybe not that simple.

Many men on the shorter side are insecure about their height. I guess for the most part (obvious or not) we have been socialized to believe that men are supposed to be the taller, more muscular and physically stronger of the sexes- as if they are naturally born physical protectors of the species. In my experience, men still believe they are supposed to be physically bigger, which includes being taller. As a result, a lot of (shorter) men set their online dating settings to filter out any women who are taller than they are.

I learned that my 5'4" stature is very pleasing to men. This was a real eye-opener to me because there was a time I had wished I were a bit taller. But here's what really concerns me... *we won't consider dating someone because of their height?* It seems rather ridiculous. I think of that tall super model who is sitting at home not getting asked out on a date. Now men are intimidated by her beauty AND her height. If she's also really smart she's going to be single forever.

Online dating is also a place in which weight is equated in. In setting up a profile, one is supposed to identify not only their height, but also their body type. *Are you slim? Do you have an athletic body type? Petite? A few extra pounds on? A lot of extra pounds on?*

Again, if you're answering truthfully it involves making a fair assessment about your own body, which we aren't always good at. We may also feel like we don't know where we belong- perhaps someone is slim but also athletic. I really struggled with this question. *How did I define my body? How would others define it? If I don't choose well, will I be filtered out of searches and lose the chance to meet the love of my life?*

Lucky for me, I must have chosen the right settings. Thanks to a little loserish technology, we did find each other.

REPARTNERING WITH JUST THE RIGHT RECIPE

I don't find it surprising that so many people settle into relationships that are not ideal for them. It takes a lot of patience to find the "right" person, and you're often left wondering if that person will ever come along. I count myself extremely lucky that I was able to finally find that person, and that our timing and availability worked out.

We clicked from the beginning. It was effortless. He was such a compliment to my life that once we had met I couldn't imagine him not being a part of it. There was never any question.

My lurking insecurities can still find their way out at times, but he puts them to rest with ease. I trust him more than anyone I have ever trusted before, more than even myself. When he tells me he believes I can do something, I believe him. When he tells me I'm beautiful, I know he truly thinks I am beautiful.

In the past I felt a certain standard to maintain, like I was supposed to be some kind of pretty accessory on a man's arm. This relationship feels different. I'm sure a big part of this is the wisdom I've gained with age and experience, and having to rely on other things rather than physical attractiveness. While I still like to look put-together and attractive, it isn't for him- I do it for *me*.

Obviously my face varies whether I have makeup on or not, but my eyes are still the same. He loves those eyes and I love his. I love that his eyes will be a constant. I love that as we age our eyes will remain the same.

If either of us get glaucoma, I'm going to be so mad.

I still sometimes struggle with my size. I was always a petite person. Over the past few years I've gained more weight than I'm comfortable with on my small frame. The combination of joint issues and pain, changing metabolism, decreased muscle tone and poor digestion have not been good for the waistline.

So, my weight crept up. It's become a challenge for me because clothing doesn't fit right, and I'm not physically comfortable. Having gained weight on my bust and rear, I'd often joke with my partner about being "all boobs and ass."

He has never once complained about my boobs and ass. But, he's pretty small statured for a man, which I found a bit intimidating in the beginning (because I feel like I'm supposed to be the smaller one). Again, my issue, not his.

One day, I was struggling with my bosom, saying "I'm not used to these," jumping up and down to make sure they were well-contained in my new bathing suit top.

He immediately stopped what he was doing and focused all his attention on me. Looking at me purposefully, but with confusion he said "but that's the way I've always known you. I've been with you for 2 years and you've always had big boobs. I don't understand why you still aren't used to them."

Oh. I hadn't considered this, but it was true. He hadn't known me when I was more slender. It wasn't as if BOOM! I woke up a year into our relationship and had gained 20lbs. My boobs had been somewhat big that entire time. Oh.

OH.

Somehow I had continued to be in denial that whole time. I was not as petite as I had been pre-40's. He clearly wasn't going to have an issue with my bountiful booty or boobs because that's how he had always known me to be. Again, this was an issue of how I identified and not being able to adapt to my changed body.

I don't believe we should rely on others to mend our insecurities. Depending on someone else to like yourself gets into dangerous territory. But I'd be lying if I said he didn't help me be more comfortable with who I am. When he assured me that this is the body he fell in love with and it is perfect the way it is, it helped calm that uneasiness.

I've learned to be more gentle with myself and not to speak ill of my parts. I realized it bothered him when I would speak negatively about myself, like I didn't believe or trust him or I questioned his judgement. My negative mumbling would be met with statements from him like "hey, don't talk about your bum like that. I love it."

Damn. He has a way with words. And I realized that likewise, I wouldn't like it if he talked negatively about any of his parts, because I love them all as they are.

※ ※ ※

I had been a huge reader in my younger days and had loved fiction. But as I grew older and my brain became more tired (and my time became more limited) I stopped reading fiction altogether. Any of my reading thus was focused around professional development, true stories about resilience, and occasionally something from the self-help genre.

On one of our first dates, he took me to a grassy spot close to the water. We laid down on the grass, and he started reading one of his favourite works of fiction to me. It was an incredible way to get to know him and what he connected to. We've enjoyed this time of reading together so much that we've kept doing it over the past 2 and a half years that we've been together.

One day, I chose a book that I felt would be more fitting for me to read (not fiction, of course). We made an exception and I read this book to him. There's a scene in the book in which the main character is involved in nude modelling. Like so many other things we've read or watched together, it led to a discussion. I told him that I've felt a calling for many years to go to a nude beach and be there... naked. I don't want to be there with anyone I know, just strangers. I feel like it would be incredibly liberating to *just be me-* comfortable in my own skin, as I should be.

I'm not sure why this feels so beautifully raw to me. And courageous. Not that being naked should be considered courageous. But it does.

I've never envisioned doing this nude beach expedition with a partner. I think there's a fear that a partner would see other women and be attracted to them, or find their bodies to be more pleasing than mine. After all, I'm not 20 anymore. I'd prefer to avoid any possible comparisons or situations that could make my insecurities come out. Of course, if I voiced this concern to him I'd be met with that look that says *what?? You are foolish for even thinking that. I only have eyes for you.*

Yes, I've seen that look. He's very good at conveying it.

I went ahead and told him I that I wanted to do the nude beach thing... and he encouraged it of course.

The funny thing is, we are both non risk-takers, introverted and modest. The thought of us going to a nude beach is quite a stretch.

We haven't had access to a nude beach as of yet. However, we did manage to have a little private skinny dip. While the teenagers were all settled into the rental cabin and behaving, we snuck out for a short kayak ride at night. While down the river, we pulled over and stripped for a midnight swim. We were giddy like a couple of teenagers who had never been naked before. It was anything but sexy- we were slipping and sliding so much in the mud that we couldn't even manage to walk without falling. But, while it was a bit of a fail, we were able to cross that off our bucket list of risqué things to do.

It's not a very long list.

Upon returning from our kayak ride, the kids were wondering why we were so wet. We made up an absurd story about an eagle swooping down on us, and tipping the boat... using arm motions and actions to make it even more dramatic. We aren't sure whether they believed it, but they stopped asking questions. Perhaps they suspected that it was better they not know.

※ ※ ※

As the summer was coming to an end, I reminded him about our plans to find a nude beach. My daughter was in the room, and gave a questionable look.
"You can't go," I said to her.
Without hesitation she replied "I'm ok with that."

※ ※ ※

I have a lot of quirks. A lot. My partner must really love me because he puts up with all of them. Yup, somehow I've managed to find the most patient person in the world to partner up with.

I've performed a very strange ritual with dressing since I was younger; when I get dressed, I like to get dressed alone. But, it's not what you may think- it's not about not wanting someone to see my body. I've gotten over that whole being naked thing with him. I'm naked in the dark, naked in the light.... Even naked in natural DAYLIGHT. Yea, you heard me. That takes guts.

I like to get dressed alone because I can be so indecisive about the outfit and what I'm going to match together that I don't want anyone to see this indecisiveness. I think it stems back to when I was younger and was upset trying on clothes, and I'd try to hide this. I feel dumb trying on clothes and changing them excessively. So, when I go into our bedroom after showering, I often instinctively close and lock the door.

It gives me that little barrier, so I'm not looking too distraught when he or someone else walks in.

Of course, since I do unlock the door and let him in, he asks why I still do this. I've tried to explain. I know it doesn't really make sense, but my mirror critique *(can I see my flab roll with this top and this pair of jeans?)* is a personal matter that I don't want to share. Luckily he is patient and can tolerate my quirks. Since he's allowed to see me naked in daylight, there are no complaints.

* * *

I once showed my partner the picture of a woman on a magazine cover. What drew me to the photo was that unlike most, her photo wasn't touched-up. There it was: her natural body, cellulite, and stretch marks. And she was beautiful. I told him why I appreciated the photo.

"But you don't have any cellulite," he said matter-of-factly.

"WHAT?!??!"

I think the neighbors down the street even heard my astonishment.

I initially thought he was just trying to spare my feelings. I've accepted the fact that I'm in my 40's and I, like other women my age, get cellulite. If he doesn't like it, then-

He argued back that I have no cellulite.

Now, this is a very smart man. Smart enough to never say something hurtful, but also smart enough to see cellulite. Again, he calmly said "honey, you have NO cellulite."

I paused, still in disbelief, but not wanting to make him feel ridiculous with my doubt. Then I slowly ventured into those waters.

"Do you know what cellulite looks like?"

"Yes," he said firmly, but not phased. "I know what cellulite looks like. Even if you did have it, I don't find it that bad."

At that point, I didn't know if he was blind or dumb. But I was pretty sure that he was the best man in the entire universe.

So, I kept staring at him in disbelief. Then I was overcome with a sense of warmth. He really thinks I don't have cellulite, or not enough worth noting. He thinks I'm a beautiful vessel…

I'm convinced that some men have blinders on when a woman is naked in front of them. They see a bum, they see hips, they see boobs, a face they find pretty, and that's all that they visually need.

He continued to talk about how my bum is adorable. "Perfection," he said.

God, I love him.

I was still soaking up the previous part of the conversation, so I didn't fully appreciate his little side ramble about my butt, until I heard him mention a dimple. He described it as a "cute dimple."

"ONE??!?!!?" I said.

By this point I was thinking this one particular dimple must be crater-sized, since he didn't notice any other cellulite or dimpling.

There was a time that someone pointing out a dimple on my bum would have set me on a downward spiral of loathing. But he was talking about it with such love, like it gave me more character. So, the comment didn't bother me at all.

A few weeks later I was getting in the shower and I turned and caught a glimpse of what I believe to be that dimple in the mirror. When I saw it, I smiled.

SMILED.

I guess an ass dimple isn't too bad if your partner thinks it's adorable.

FORTY-THREE

Forty-three years old.
I felt as though I'd come a long way. I knew I had. But maybe not as far as I'd thought.

I showered and got dressed for the day. I chose a pair of very pale pink jeans with a lot of stretch, a greyish tank top with lace detail, and a purple/plum top that wraps and ties. The outfit was well thought-out. The pants, almost white but not quite.... (I'm a poet)...fit in with the beautiful day and the sunshine. They felt and looked quite "spring." It was a good week in terms of my belly issues, so I would be able to wear the fitted jeans without too much discomfort.

The (layering) tank has become one of my wardrobe staples. In fact, I have a huge bin of tank tops. I tell our daughters that if they ever need a tank top, come borrow one, because I certainly have what they need. Every color, different styles... some with spaghetti straps, some with thick straps. Some have lace on the top, some have lace on the bottom. The purpose of the tank – in case you are a man and don't know this- is to help cover our "problem areas." I no longer wear short tops, so a tank with a pretty lace bottom can help cover my belly (should my top garment ride up). It also has a key role in disguising a bountiful booty. When the tank is long, it covers the top part of one's bum, making not so much bum visible. The key is finding tank tops that are long enough to properly do all this.

As an aside... long tanks are also handy to wear when

you're young and have gotten a tattoo on your back/waist area and don't want your parents to see it. Just don't make the mistake that I did and have your father stand behind you at the car as you lean over and buckle your child into their car seat. My rather conservative father took it well. Although I did later find a box that said "tattoo removal kit" sitting on the bed, containing sanders and other ouchy tools. I enjoy my father's sense of humour.

After the birth of my 3rd child, I discovered the beauty of the wrap dress. You can fluctuate in weight, change in shape... they hug your body and show off your curves. They look good at any weight. Seriously. It's like they accentuate all the good things, and hug your waist, making it look smaller.

I still own that dress, 13 years later. It's a jersey material, more comfortable than wearing pajamas. No uncomfortable waistband. Navy. I usually wear it to funerals. I should probably start wearing it to other things; it feels wrong when I get a little excited to pull out that comfortable dress because I'm going to a funeral.

So, I had been on the hunt for 13 years for other wrap garments. Sweaters, tops, skirts and dresses. The fashion industry hasn't caught on that they look great on all body types, because they can be really hard to find. Much to my delight, I discovered one retailer (in the mall) that has embraced the wrap trend. And they have an online store, with free return shipping. Let's just say, I ordered quite a number of items upon this discovery. I also returned quite a number of items, but I kept a super cute pair of pants and the plum wrap long-sleeved shirt. It minimizes my bust a bit, shows off my waist, and because it's not long, I layer it with a long tank to minimize my rear end. It was that wrap shirt that I was wearing on this fateful day when I was forty-three.

I made the mistake of looking in a full-length mirror before I left the house.

I know... I know...

There's something about white or almost white pants. They

aren't slimming (as opposed to black or navy, which *are* slimming). I knew it was a risk even buying these pants in the first place, but I had had a moment of insanity and bought them. Now I was questioning my choice. Keep in mind, these were stretchy and very, very tight.

Back to the mirror...

My butt was huge.

From the front, everything looked ok except that I could see how big my thighs were with the way they were fitting. Those thighs were not muscle. They were fat. I don't mind a bum and some curvy thighs on another woman, but I struggle with it on myself.

It just looked all wrong. It looked like my ass never ended. Like, it was bountiful and round, but also flat and continuous. Seemingly not possible, but it was. I immediately thought the pants should be navy. And perhaps in the clothing donation bin.

To make things worse, I couldn't find my seamless underwear, which I know is a necessity for wearing these pants. And to make things super worse, the underwear I was wearing was stretchy and had hole details in it. Of course, during that moment I had an epiphany- if you can see simple underwear lines, you can probably see the texture of all these hole things on my butt too. And so, I bent over, examined closely, confirmed this to be true, and wondered how dumb I could be that I hadn't realized this before. Now, I had a huge, textured ass. And the texture would draw even more attention to it.

Then the negative self-talk started. Or what we could rightly call: self-induced emotional abuse.

How is my ass still this big? That's disgusting. I hate the way these pants hug my thighs.

In that moment, when I looked at my textured, massive, light pink never-ending ass, I felt disgusted. That's the feeling I felt, disgust. And annoyed. Because I had made a ton of dietary changes for medical reasons, and I hadn't lost weight.

Then I had thoughts of my partner, and felt guilt because I was disrespecting something he loves so much.

He loves this ass. He thinks it's attractive. I love this about him. But, why does he?

Well, I did what any defiant, trying-to-love-oneself woman would do. I told the thoughts to go screw themselves. I was not changing again. So, out I went to do errands. With my hole-y undies and textured butt. If anyone noticed, they likely thought the texture was the ripples from massive cellulite coming through.

Who the heck designs underwear with hole details?

In an effort to detract attention from my seemingly over-cellutitey ass, I decided to make a change with my face. I immediately booked an appointment at one of those "classy" salons that offers an array of services that I had never heard of. Being tired of the maintenance involved with my sparse eyebrows, I thought that getting them filled in and dyed with henna sounded like a practical and ingenious idea. After all, the salon's website convinced me that my brows would look great and my routine would become effortless. I was very optimistic and excited for the upcoming results (which I should know by now is usually a very bad sign).

The women in the salon were living advertisements, with their defined, crisp eyebrows. I told the aesthetician that I trusted her, thinking that this sharing of confidence would help contribute to a positive result.

Note to self: never trust someone else with my eyebrows.

With the dying process complete, the technician broke it to me that the henna didn't take to my skin, which meant I would still need to fill in the gaps and shape them. So, why did I just spend...??

In an attempt to make them a bit more presentable, she waxed them to clean them up a little (which yes, she also charged me for). The big reveal showed a less than ideal outcome: the hair was super dark, while the sparse parts didn't hold the pigment. They appeared worse than before I had walked into the salon, but I did what I always do in these situations-I shoved my feelings of disappointment deep down, mustered up a smile, thanked her, (paid- grr), and left the salon.

By that time, I had learned that a failed attempt to makeover something on my body wasn't the end of the world. I held myself together and drove to the nearby pharmacy that has a cosmetics person on staff. I told her where I had just been and what had transpired. I gently begged for help and in my vulnerability I told her that I was giving myself completely over to her.

Note to self: remember the previous note to self.

At that point, she should have told me she wasn't a miracle worker.

But she didn't. Instead, she collected up a few products and worked on one brow, leaving the other as it was when I first came in. Then she showed me.

WOAH.

Like, WOAH.

They were dark. Very dark.

"You don't think that's a good color? Really?" she asked, surprised.

Ah, no. And they still didn't look crisp like I had wanted them. They looked quite like the dollar store moustaches we had bought for my partner when the kids and I dressed him up for Halloween as a 70's disco star. Porn 'stache eyebrows really didn't suit me.

I asked her what product she used on her brows (they were lovely), to which she replied "oh, I paint them on."

HUH?

I hadn't realized I should have gone to the craft store rather than the cosmetic store to get my eyebrows done.

I decided to buy one of the brow pencil products she had used, minus the other product that had made them even more stark. I still was very WOAH and HUH? leaving the scene of the crime (the store). I then sat in my car, and tried as best as I could to fix the darn things. Once I felt they looked better, I drove home.

As soon as I walked into the house, my teenage daughter (who had not yet started to develop an interest in eyebrows or eye products) exclaimed, "wow! Your eyebrows are so dark!" from across the room. This is a child who doesn't notice anything, ever. I instantly knew my efforts to tame the porn 'staches had failed.

So, there I was on this ill-fated day, not only exposing myself to ridicule over my huge texture-y butt, but I also had extreme-black-not-quite-70's-porn-star-moustache eyebrows. I wasn't sure which was worse. I'm happy to report that no one screamed in terror, including my sweet partner, who is too nice (and smart) to make any seemingly negative comments about my looks.

I hope to marry him someday.

❊ ❊ ❊

A noteworthy decision…

I threw out that holey pair of underwear.

THE WEDDING DRESS – PART ONE

The smart man that he is, my guy decided to make it official and ask me to marry him. The proposal was sweet and intimate. He took me to the place that he read to me on one of our first dates. We laid on a blanket on the grass. He started reading a new book, a book he had made for me. It contained poems he had written for me, photos, and other personal things. It was absolutely perfect. There were a lot of tears.

We had talked a lot about marriage prior to this, so it wasn't a big surprise that it was coming. My views on engagements and marriage have evolved much over the past 20 years. I know legal marriage is not for everyone. I think it's meaningful if the parties involved find it to be meaningful and valuable. Not everyone does, and that's ok. It was still something each of us wanted though, to be legally married.

I also don't believe that official engagements are necessary. But, there's still a part of me that likes a formal proposal. I like knowing that someone had really thought it through and had made a solid decision about wanting to spend the rest of their life with me. Since we had to wait a bit to get married, that "engagement" step was very important to me.

Admittedly, it didn't feel like a decision for either of us. There was no question as to whether we should be together.

Once we were officially engaged, I could start looking for a dress. We wanted to keep things simple with the entire wedding, including the dress. I knew from conversations that he had envisioned his "bride" to wear a white dress. There aren't many opportunities to wear a white dress, so I was happy for the opportunity. Hopefully I could manage to pull it off without slopping food down the front of myself (before pictures at least).

My first attempt at dress shopping was a last minute decision. I had an hour and a half to waste in the city and decided it would be fun to waste it in a dress store. I went by myself to the small store. It resembled more of a discount thrown-together kind of set up than a bridal boutique. There was only one woman working. By the end of that next hour and a half, that woman knew my body almost as well as my partner did.

Modesty has no place in trying on wedding dresses. First of all, you need help. The dresses are awkward. They're big. They're fragile. In those moments, you are vulnerable and helpless.

Cinderella made it look so easy, with her fairy godmother simply waving her wand. It's not at all like that.

"Do you need some help getting it on?" she offered.

"No, I should be ok..."

A few minutes of huffing and puffing went on, with the occasional "huh?" and oh *crap, I need to be careful I don't tear the fabric*... then I offered a relenting "um... yea... I think I need your help."

You know she was likely waiting just outside the door smirking, wondering when I'd admit that I needed her help.

That's right. As hard as you might try, you eventually succumb and ask the sales woman to come help you get into the dress. And then she becomes your best friend. You wonder why you denied her in the first place.

Let me set up this scenario by stating a few facts.

1. One of the major considerations with fitting a formal dress is properly fitting the breasts.
2. Wedding dresses are typically not worn with a bra.
3. If any bra is used, one would usually opt for a strapless

bra.

4. My breasts are not of the right character anymore to successfully stay in place with a strapless bra.

5. There still exists the expectation that the bride is supposed to look good on her wedding day, taking on a great deal of attention. And of course, a bride's bosom is front and center in that attention, captured forever by countless photos.

6. Flat breasts are not the bridal look I am going for.

With these dress trials, I went right to bare breasts. So, there I was, at the dress place without any loved ones (or a bra) for support. A woman I had never met was helping me into dresses and helping me get *the girls* in there all contained. One major thing that added to fitting issues was the fact that retailers don't tend to stock wedding dresses in my size. The sample dresses are usually a fair bit larger, then they pin the dress in the back to fit your form better. (This ensures that a sample dress can fit multiple sizes as they don't keep multiple dresses in stock.) Therefore, I was trying on dresses that were all several sizes too big. There was way too much room for *the girls* to shift around and try to party.

My primary role in that hour and a half was lifting and containing my boobs while the salesperson used her enhanced skills to get me all pinned in the back. I would then toddle out to the full mirror in the waiting area to take in the magic of me in the dress, carefully trying not to spring a clothespin. I learned a few things from that dress-trying-on event.

1. *Trying on wedding dresses when you are self-conscious about parts of your body is hard.*

This would not be my first wedding. From experience, I knew I would be the centre of attention. Each time I thought of this, a private elopement sounded more and more enticing.

2. *There are less options for dresses that look really good when you don't have the breasts of a 20 year old.*

This is comparable to bathing suit shopping. If you're deflated like me, save yourself the sorrow and skip trying on strapless dresses.

3. *Mermaid-style dresses show things you don't want shown.*

Mermaid dresses are ass-hugging, belly-hugging, hug-hugging. These dresses are meant for mermaids, not humans.

4. *Wedding dresses can be very flattering to the body, as they can accentuate your chest, fit your waist nicely, and flow away from the body (provided you don't wear the mermaid style).*

If you're concerned about your bum/thighs, you may find a wedding dress to be very pleasing to the figure. I might start wearing a wedding dress regularly around the house, or while doing errands.

Having had a very petite waist before, I was very aware of my painful and bloated belly as I tried on the dresses. Some were more flattering than others. I didn't expect, however, what the sales woman would then suggest to me.

"How long is it until the wedding? Do you have time to lose weight before?"

What? Did that really happen?

I had never in my life had a person even hint that I lose weight. It was weird. I felt like I should be offended. The funny thing is, I handled it very well. I obviously had a belly. She was a mom like me (and larger than me). My belly was a fact that was, well... factual. The even more bizarre thing is that, while it was a strange conversation, it didn't trigger any deep-seeded things in my mind, or send me into a tailspin.

I guess I've come a lot further than I thought I had.

THE WEDDING DRESS – PART TWO

After I failed to find the dress I wanted on the first attempt, I booked an appointment with another bridal shop to try on dresses. It was what you'd expect from a bridal shop: beautiful building, many gorgeous selections, and very personal service. It was the kind of place that made it into an experience for the bride and her guests. There was a slim possibility that we might be able to get married in only a few months time, so I needed a dress as soon as possible to leave time for ordering and alteration.

It seemed like a fun opportunity to take a few of our kids, so I took along one of my daughters (my other daughter was not able to attend), my partner's daughter, and a friend.

There were two sales people present- the store owner and a very peppy, friendly salesman.

"So, when is your wedding date?" she questioned.

"We aren't completely certain yet, as we're waiting on a few things, but we'd prefer to get married in 3 or 4 months."

She looked alarmed.

I've never understood why the brides-to-be who are featured on reality tv shows choose dresses that barely contain their ample bosom. *Really?* They say they want to look *sexy*. I thought sexy was reserved for your partner the night of... not for all your relatives and friends to see. I could be wrong here, but I suspect not too many dads want to walk their daughter down the aisle, fearful that a boob could fall out.

That's not the look I was going for.

My goal was to look beautiful and elegant. I wanted my dress to be soft, sweet and simple, like one might see a bride wear at a beach wedding. I didn't want a train. I did want length. I didn't want it to be too full. I definitely did not want tulle. I envisioned chiffon as the outer material, because of how simply and beautifully it falls. I was certain I didn't want a strapless dress, and probably not one with spaghetti straps. I pictured it having no sleeves, and a v-neck. Very supportive in the front. The dress should be white or off white. I thought this would be an easy task.

Oh heck, no.

Maybe simple wedding dresses aren't popular this season. Or maybe they're extremely popular and they had all sold out. Despite having 5 of us pulling out sample dresses for me to try on, we were still having trouble finding dresses that didn't have a train and that were a reasonable price.

The previous trial run trying on dresses had me primed for this day. I wasn't at all worried about flashing a boob with this saleswoman.

The owner had a very effective system for helping her brides get in and out of dresses. She had a beautiful robe that she used as a cover to help with modesty, while the bride-to-be was slipping the dress on and off. She was there to do the zipping and pinning so that the dress (that was many sizes too big of course) would fit.

After going through this process, I'd walk out in the dress for feedback from my groupies.

Feedback for each dress that I modelled was mixed. The teenage girls seemed to have a pretty good sense of my style and what suited me. My friend had good input, but we clearly didn't share the same vision. She liked the mermaid/hugging style dresses, even though it was obvious that I felt stiff and I couldn't sit down or walk with ease. I was afraid I was going to bust the butt out if I sat down, or the side seams if I tried to eat something.

Again, mermaid dresses belong on mermaids, not me.

Then I tried on a dress that was simple, and had spaghetti straps (something I had assumed would not give me enough chest support). Much to my surprise, I really liked the dress. It was fitted on the top, v-neck, floor-length, chiffon… with a very nice fall to it. When I wore that one out to be previewed, the girls really liked it, whereas my friend immediately spoke up and said she didn't like it. She felt it was missing something. Point taken, but I still liked that dress.

I tried on a few other dresses that were obviously outside my price range (although, I had never really determined what that was). They were beautiful dresses, but something was off. They seemed too fancy for our casual wedding.

I went back to the dress I liked that I had tried on earlier. But before I walked back out, I pulled part of my hair up and fastened it with a decorative clip. I also carried the prop bouquet that was provided in the changing room.

The reaction changed when I walked out into their view. My daughter loved it. My soon-to-be step-daughter gasped, put her hand to her chest and teared up. That was one of the true highlights of my life. I still smile when I think of her reaction; I wish her father could have seen it.

My friend still insisted that something was missing. The boutique owner had a plan… she brought over some wee delicate belts that could be added to the dresses- ones with pearls, ones with crystals, ones with a combination of the two. That's what was missing- a little bling. My (step) daughter told me how much it complimented me. I knew her dad would think it was perfect.

I wasn't expecting to like the spaghetti straps as I had believed they wouldn't give me enough support. The dress itself gave the support so well that the straps were more decorative than anything. The top of the dress did indeed contain my breasts well. I wouldn't have to worry about them flattening or falling out with everyone watching.

I also loved how flattering the dress was to my waist, then fell gently down past my feet. Simple, elegant. And the ironic thing? It was by far the least expensive of the dresses. I hadn't know that before I fell in love with it, but it did make it even a bit more perfect.

It was my dress.

Then there was cause for celebration! They brought campaign for us older folk, and sparkling juice for the younger ones. They took a picture, to forever capture our happiness. I went to pay and order my actual dress. The owner entered my measurements into the computer, which then suggested what size (in that style) would best fit me. (Of course, the seamstress would make it fit perfect later.) I was stunned by the suggested size. It was a larger size than anything I had ever worn. Guess those days of smaller sizes were done.

At least she didn't suggest I lose weight.

Then I did what every woman who has worked through a lot of her body issues does: I reminded myself that it's not the size that matters, it's the fit. No one is going to ask the dress size. No one is going to care. I looked sweet, and my breasts looked damn good in that dress, so that was all that the groom would care about. And just like that, I paid for my dress with a smile on my face.

❈ ❈ ❈

Months later, after getting the call, I went back to the bridal boutique to try on my dress. Much to our surprise, it was even bigger than the sample size that I had tried on.

"Did you lose weight?" she asked.

"Not at all," I answered.

Hmm...

This was a problem. I signed off on the size when the dress was ordered. We had been expecting it to be altered, but there's only so much that a dress can be taken in.

"This doesn't fit my boobs right," I noted aloud. This was a definite problem. That was the best part of the dress on me. The groom was not going to like that.

"How much time do you have before the wedding?" she queried.

By that time we knew the wedding wouldn't be until the summer, quite some time away.

"Quite awhile. It's not until July."

She offered to order another size in, saying she could keep that one in the store to sell. Fantastic service. I was relieved that I wouldn't need to gain 20 lbs on my chest in order to have the dress fit properly.

DRESS CODES AND SCANDALOUS TITTIES

For as long as human beings have worn clothing, there have been expectations of how they would dress, depending on the situation. This includes work (which varies depending on workplace), home, church, school, social gatherings, and ceremonies. For whatever reason, our gender has always dictated the specifics of that written or unwritten code.

I suspect there have been women in every time period who have balked at dress expectations. Contrary to what the patriarchy wanted us to believe in the past, women are smart. We've known that dress serves a purpose, an oppressive one at that. Dress has helped keep women "in their place", modesty being forced upon us in terms of covering our entire bodies, our hair, sometimes our faces. We've been encouraged to wear restrictive things like hooped dresses, corsets, and shoes that stunt our feet's growth, in the name of "beauty" and social class identification. Above all else, we should always look pretty.

They denied us pockets in our clothing for FAR too long. If that doesn't say gender oppression, I don't know what does.

Dress codes also serve to give both men and women an expectation of behaviour, serving another purpose in our history. We make assumptions about behaviour based on whether someone is wearing a suit, a wedding dress, a knee-length skirt and heels, a military uniform. Our dress influences how others perceive us.

Those who work in offices or the teaching profession tend to appreciate their "dress down days", only to be told that on most days they can't wear jeans, for risk of being viewed as less professional. *Is it fair to judge someone's job performance or professionalism by the style of pants they wear?*

As time has gone on, we've come to question the relevancy of dress codes, and things have slowly relaxed. Women are permitted to wear pants. (Although some religious groups still require that women wear dresses or skirts.) Jeans have become acceptable to wear on occasion at some workplaces. People don't tend to dress as formal for funerals. Church congregations are encouraging patrons to concentrate more on worship than focusing on wearing one's "Sunday best." We still gravitate to wearing traditional garb around anything ceremonious, I presume due to our tendency to enjoy formality and anything that provokes feelings of nostalgia.

Still, we have dress codes. Yes, there are expectations for men too (such as not wearing a sleeveless shirt in the workplace). But arguably, women still fare much worse when it comes this. Why?

Boobs.

Well, not just boobs. But largely boobs. Even though half of the population has (or will have at some point) breasts, they still make people uncomfortable. You'd think that everyone would be pretty accustomed to having them around by now.

* * *

In our school zone, there was (perhaps still is) a rule that girls cannot wear spaghetti straps to school. In fact, all shirt or dress straps had to be at least 3 fingers wide. Do you know how ridiculous I felt shopping, trying to find spring/summer dresses for my elementary-aged, pre-pubescent daughter, that were 3 finger widths or more?

Why must the straps be 3 fingers wide? To hide a bra strap? (ah, the scandalous bra strap...) Is it because spaghetti straps don't always provide a lot of support for a bigger bosom? Are they afraid someone's shirt is going to burst open and someone could lose an eye?

What happens if a teenage girl doesn't wear a bra to school? No, seriously. What is the proper etiquette on that one?

It's been hard to enforce school dress codes in these parts. For starters, teachers are teaching. They have a very limited amount of time in their day; their top priority is *not* calling out dress code violations for visible bra straps. Most of the male teachers I know would not be comfortable calling out a teenage girl for a dress code violation. As for the female teachers, the ones I've spoken with don't wish to enforce a practice that's often thought to be sexist and essentially body shaming.

Regulating what girls wear in school has always gotten under my skin. I'm always tempted to push this a little every time I need to go to the high school. I daydream about putting on a pair of cut-off Daisy Duke shorts and a skimpy, spaghetti-strapped crop-top. Or a string bikini, two sizes too small. Some day. Some day...

※ ※ ※

Sometimes I wonder... in places where female toplessness is commonplace (at beaches for instance), are breasts considered to be sexual in the bedroom? Or do they become as ignored as a pair of elbows?

I'm not certain our part of the world is ready to de-sexualize breasts. Isn't there a good portion of our population that *likes* breasts being sexualized? I'm not saying that women want to be nastily ogled in public, but *aren't there plenty of men and women who enjoy thinking breasts are sexy behind closed doors?*

Provided we want to continue moving towards not hypersexualizing breasts, what will it take for our North American thinking to evolve?

I consider myself to be a critical thinker, and not one to support any ideology that serves to oppress women. But, I still struggle with the concept of nudity and sexuality. In fact, around 25 years ago, I wrote a research paper about the social construction of nudity and sexuality for a religious studies course I was taking in university. It was probably one of my best assignments during my academic career. However, it's one thing to research it and critically reflect on it, and another thing to live it. And now have daughters living it.

I am against body shaming. I have nudes of women framed on my wall; I think the female form is lovely in all shapes. I've never hidden nude bodies from my children (unless of course they were engaged in a sexual act). I believe it to be sexist and a complete double standard that men get to show their bare chests and women cannot.

But…

Am I really ready to free the female nipple?

(I'm not sure why I singularized nipple there, as they do typically come in pairs.)

I want to be ready. I wish we lived in a place and time that showing a breast wasn't scandalous. Where we could go topless at any beach if we wanted to. When we could strip down on scorching hot days while mowing the lawn, like our penised counterparts. I want that. But the truth is, I am a product of my time. I grew up in a generation that embraced modesty and not showing one's chest. I also grew up in a time that only "perfect" breasts were put out there to be viewed, for which I have never thought of my own as. So as much as I would like for the female nipple to find its freedom, I am unlikely myself to start doing yard work topless. But, as strange as this might sound to those my age, I do hope that someday breasts have lost their hypersexualization and my daughters or great granddaughters have this option. And that they wear plenty of sunscreen while doing so, of course.

* * *

After hashing all of this around in my brain, I realized that what really matters in all of this is how our young people feel. After all, I don't believe my generation handled this whole dress thing as best as we could have. So, I asked a few teenage girls to simply tell me what they think about having a dress code in school. I've known from past conversations that most girls seem to be against it, but I wanted to know specifically why.

"The problem is that nudity and the body are overly sexualized, when they shouldn't be," one explained.

I agree very much with this point. Although, as I detailed previously, there is a complexity to this since our society hasn't yet embraced being comfortable with the naked human body. We're only now just finally normalizing a woman's breastfeeding of her baby in public, a natural process that should (I think) hold no shame or stigma.

"I think people should be able to wear whatever they want to wear," the same young woman added.

Another said "I think it's sexist. If your reason for a dress code is it distracts the boys, you need to educate your boys on how to treat women and control themselves and not shame young girls away from wearing tank tops and shorts."

That's right. It should not be a girl's responsibility to ensure that her male peers are not too distracted to obtain their education. I particularly appreciated her wording with "you need to educate your boys." Yes parents. It starts with us. It seems that most of the "education" we've received has been in the form of telling girls to cover up and how to dress. This mirrors the education that my generation had been given around sexual assault: teaching girls how to avoid getting sexually assaulted, rather than teaching boys that in no circumstance is it ok to sexually assault someone.

We need to stop telling females that it's their fault for being ogled, harassed and assaulted.

One of the young women I spoke with also brought up a point that I've struggled to define:

"As long as you're covering what should be covered by a bathing suit it should be fine. Clearly if someone is showing up in a stripper's outfit to school, someone should be called... but I've had friends get sent home for wearing long-sleeved shirts with the shoulders cut out."

A-ha.

There's a line. There is always a line, otherwise some kids would be showing up to school in the nude. But, *who decides that line? Who enforces it? Why is it there? What is the purpose?*

The problem with the line (drawn somewhere between fully-covered dress and full-on nudity) is that the line is different for everyone. The line is affected by personal, religious, generational, and cultural influences.

Which brings me to the realization yet again that there is no easy fix or solution that will satisfy everyone. I think it's important however to be mindful that these dress codes have tended to be more centred around keeping a woman's body "modest." Any dress code that shames a female's body is not ok.

Yup, we've got boobs and ass. Get over it.

※ ※ ※

I look ahead to the future... We have no dress codes. Girls are wearing crop tops, showing bras. Then they don't wear bras... then eventually, no shirts. Because you know, we've successfully managed to de-sexualize breasts. There are posters on the walls of the schools, saying: Breasts are nothing to be ashamed of- release your ta-tas! Then we decide that genitalia aren't shameful too. Eventually no one is wearing pants to school. (Parents are happy because there is less laundry.) On the hot days, sweaty teenagers are slipping off chairs at an alarming rate. Head injuries increase. No one goes out at lunch for fresh air anymore, because they keep getting sunburns on their winkly-dinks and hoo-has. All fast food places within walking distance of the schools close down, because of lack of business. The economy suffers and we go into a recession.

THOUGHTS IN THE DENTAL CHAIR

I'm not sure what other people think about while in the dental chair, but these are some thoughts that have run through my head. There's something about having someone (that I'm not in a close relationship with) in my face that can be unsettling to me...

Why did I eat that garlic bread for lunch?
Do I have a lot of acne right now?
Do I have on a shirt that they can see down?
Did I brush ok?
Did I blend my concealer well?
Why are they making me wear these stupid glasses?
I wonder what I look like in these stupid glasses?
Do my eyebrows look bad this close-up?
Is there pepper in my teeth?
Am I covered in dog hair?
Why did I eat something that would make me so gassy?
Why didn't I wear socks?
Should I have exfoliated my dry face?
How yellow are my teeth?
What was the point of me foolishly wearing lipstick?
Does she realize I'm enviously looking at her fantastic eyelashes?
Does my hair have sprinkles?
If I fart right now, will they hear it over the drill?

Did I remember to wear deodorant?
DO THEY EVEN CARE ABOUT ANY OF THIS???

Can I stay in this comfortable reclined chair all day? Ahhhh...

SHOPPING: TRUSTING THE SALES ASSOCIATE

It was a hot summer's day in early July. The birds were chirping, the sun was shining, and everything that wasn't completely indestructible was melting. We had just driven to a neighbouring province in preparation for an appointment at the children's hospital. By "we", I mean my teenage son, his caregiver and myself.

It was not our first trip to the children's hospital. In fact, we had made many a trip, and it would certainly not be our last. I prefer making the drive in the non-winter months because it gives more daylight hours for driving. The hospital is about 4.5 hrs away from home. Some would measure less, but I tend to stay within the speed limit, and factor in time for a few pee breaks.

Actually, there are other pit stops I make as well:
- coffee
- candy
- fast food
- feeding my son
- paying the darn pay toll and peeing
- shopping
- taking pictures with Bunny (Bunny is a stuffed bunny that

I take photos of for my daughter when I'm away, doing various things... ordering fast food, visiting landmarks, having a bath with a glass of wine...)
- getting gas
- getting stuck in construction, detoured, and crying

It can take anywhere between 4.5-9 hours for me to make the trip.

To say I have a terrible sense of direction would be an understatement. As such, I don't stray far from the intended course. I also have this thing where (because there is no guaranteed parking where we usually lodge) I drive straight to the children's hospital, park, and then begin the trek on foot to the place we stay. Well, here's the thing: we have to carry all of our things for that walk. My son needs a lot. Not just his clothes, but his medications, special food, and all his supplies. Then there's my clothes, toiletries, water, candy... Unfortunately my sweet teenage boy (who uses a wheelchair) can't help carry what we need. I usually load a bag or two onto the back of his chair, strap a very over-packed and heavy backpack onto my back (sometimes with Bunny peeking out) and proceed to push the wheelchair all the way to the lodge. Not such a great plan for someone who has joint issues, is it? Doing this in the winter can be problematic because sidewalks with ice and snow are not wheelchair friendly. Pushing my son and dragging all this gear in the hot months is problematic because I feel like I'm going to pass out from the heat.

On this particular hot, sticky July day, my son's caregiver had the pleasure of sharing the walk with us.

She is a godsend. She helps carry the things we need. But, she's more than just a pack mule. She keeps him content for medical tests, gives me breaks, and shares duties through the night (which is especially helpful if he decides not to sleep).

While we were walking the several blocks from the van that day, her sandal started to break. This posed a real problem because we had packed as light as possible and she hadn't brought any extra footwear. We were going to be on-foot for a few days (walking back and forth as we were staying a few nights), so the sandals were obviously not going to make it.

Naturally, that meant we had to go shopping.

I didn't want to drive from my secured parking spot to the mall, so we decided to take the city bus. I had never used the wheelchair option on a city bus (we don't live in the city) and was very eager to see how this process worked. ALL the city busses had this ability, which is a big deal when you're not used to having such good wheelchair accessibility.

We got to the mall without great incident (although getting back was an entirely different story). Upon walking into the shopping centre, I heard what I can only believe was a choir of angels breaking into beautiful song. The mall was multi-levelled, and there seemed to be endless stores that we didn't have at home. The Victoria's Secret store took up pretty much a whole wing! I'm sorry to disappoint, but I didn't try on anything at Victoria's Secret. However, I did like the variety I saw from a distance and would consider going in another time. Surely there would be something there that could accentuate all my womanly features.

I did, however, make the mistake of wandering into a few stores that I shouldn't have entered. I was apparently in the designated luxury clothing wing. Fabrics interwoven with gold flakes...

I bet the sales staff get a good chuckle out of those who enter the store, and then panic and try to leave without drawing attention to themselves. I was one of those people.

I have yet to master the art of discretely leaving a store after catching a glimpse of the prices. So, it was awkward. I froze. I tried to keep my facial position neutral. I backed up slowly, out of the store. This happened at several retail stores in this wing, until I smartened up and left. Because I have a mortgage to pay.

Have you ever looked online for a place to eat, and it shows you how pricey the restaurant is? On the scale, $ is low.... $$$$ is very expensive. Why do they not have those signs outside clothing stores? Or maybe a defibrillator to jumpstart a heart again when someone has gone into shock?

The angels' voices redirected me. I saw a store that was familiar! One that I had previous history with, GOOD history! They had nice clothes at reasonable prices.

Of course, I went in.

I'm happy to report that I had a very good experience in that store. I did not sulk in the changing room. I didn't engage in negative self-talk. Even when clothing didn't look quite as I hoped it would on my body, I didn't let it discourage me. I found a few items that were different from my usual colors and styles that I considered adding to my wardrobe.

I bit the bullet and actively enlisted a salesperson to help me find items that went together. In this particular store, the salespeople were all 18ish young women. Perky young women don't have stretched-out bellies or blubby thighs. They were likely unable to relate to my body woes, or such was my assumption. I suppose it's unfair to think that 18 year olds who work in fashion don't get hung up on their own body insecurities. I certainly had my insecurities at that age.

I gave in to my reservations and decided to speak openly and put my trust into the salesperson. Let's call her Jane.

In the past, I have bought articles of clothing that I like, but didn't already own a "match" to accompany it. The problem was, I'd get the item home, and intend to buy that other "right" piece of clothing to go with it, then it would never happen. I've come to the conclusion that I either HAVE to already own something I know will work with the piece, or make sure I find that piece in the store and leave with a complete outfit.

This was the problem I was facing at this time, especially with the new "paper bag" style shorts that I fell in love with – no top to go with them. They were a dressy material, had a striped pattern with a beautiful coral color, didn't wrinkle easily, had a flattering tie waist and were ON SALE. Bonus. Zero guilt.

The paper bag style, if you are not familiar with, sits fitted at your waist (usually tied, I believe), with the bottom part tending to be a bit more flowy or loose. Above the waist the material looks to be a bit gathered or cinched, sometimes ruffled. I'm guessing it's called a paper bag style because you might liken it to what a paper bag would look like if you took a bag and scrunched it together, like people do when they are hyperventilating and need to breath into a bag. Like when you go into those clothing stores with the hefty price tags and it takes your breath away. (I think they should give out paper bags upon entry to the $$$$ stores.)

The thing that threw me off a bit with these shorts is that you can't wear them with a shirt that goes down over the top, because a shirt won't sit flat with the gathered part underneath. If you did, it would cover the cute detailing of the shorts/pants (which is the entire point to wearing these), and you'd have a lot of bunchy material bulging around your mid-section. Not cute. In this case, it would be best to wear a bodysuit or shirt that is tucked in. The other option would be to wear a shirt that is short and stops before the top of the shorts. That's getting into dangerous territory for a woman in her 40's who had previously carried three big babies in her belly.

But I really, really liked these shorts.

I tasked Jane with finding a shirt in the store that I would be able to pair with them. I had also found a very cute form-fitting skirt that I was determined to find a shirt for. Jane took on that job too. The skirt was easier to find something to go with, as it covered my belly and I could simply find a matching form-fitted top to go with it. She came through on finding one. The result was pretty flattering, so I was pleased.

Finding a top to accompany the paper bag shorts was a little more complicated. But Jane, having all that youthful energy, was up for the job. She was incredible. I explained what I was looking for and why, and wasn't too embarrassed to explain (after all, *why should I be?*) She came back with a great selection of items for me to try.

A word from the wise: if you're going clothing shopping, always make sure you wear good underwear, otherwise you can't see what something will properly look like on you. But, I hadn't planned on this shopping expedition; I had packed for the children's hospital, not for the fashion runway. I was wearing horrid shorts style underwear that had weird lines and did not present well on my butt when trying on tight skirts. I also realized that the comfortable bra I was wearing- the one that I had thought was decent- was anything but. I felt obligated to tell her I hadn't planned for this, hence the poor underwear decision. Maybe I should have gone to Victoria's Secret first.

Jane pulled through; I purchased the skirt, shorts and two tops that went with them. I also purchased a thin fabric white shirt that tied at the waist, which I confidently stated aloud that it made my boobs look good. She did not confirm nor deny this statement.

That white shirt looks great with a pair of jeans I have. My partner later agreed that it's very flattering on the chest, so it was clearly a sound investment. I just have to remember to wear a good bra with it.

* * *

On the way back to our home province after the hospital appointment, we stopped in a town for lunch. I remembered that there was a clothing store there that I liked. And so, we went shopping. Again.

I found the cutest little comfy camouflage dress for summer. Dresses are my favourite. One piece of clothing. You don't have to worry about matching pieces, or part of an outfit being in the dirty laundry pile. Dresses are ideal for lazy or unorganized people, which is ironic because I often hear "oh, why are you dressed up today?"

"I'm just lazy and this is more comfortable than pajamas," is my go-to response.

That's right. They don't dig into my belly, which I avoid like the plague due to my abdominal issues. They're roomy, which is ideal for overeating at Thanksgiving and Christmas. When my guy doesn't have room to eat that piece of pie after that full holiday meal... guess what?!?! I've got loads of expansion room.

When buying the camo dress, I found a sweet pair of rose gold-colored sandals that were somewhat dressy (more than my usual flip flops). They were slightly elevated, with no heel- perfect, since I can't wear heels due to my unstable joints. This particular store chain gives names to their shoes- and this pair happened to share our daughter's name. Plus they were on sale. The angels were providing signs everywhere to let me know I should buy these sandals. So, I did.

Needless to say, I went home pretty happy with my wardrobe. And because my daughter (the only one of the 4 girls who can fit into some of my clothes) was away for the summer, I didn't lose any of my new clothes to her. For a few weeks, anyway.

SHOPPING: THE BOUNCE TEST

My teenage daughter that I just mentioned… let's call her Jane #2… she needed to go shopping for a few things before she went away. Specifically, she needed bras, underwear, and a bathing suit. As a rule, she doesn't like to shop, which I really don't understand. Lucky for me, she really needed these things, so she abstained from the usual reluctance and was positive about it.

In other words, she didn't complain excessively like teenagers do.

Upon entering the store, we were greeted by my future sister-in-law. Let's call her Jane #3. I had forgotten that she worked there. She's very down-to-earth and I like her, so I knew that I would be comfortable with her helping me. I knew *I* would be comfortable; the question is… *would Jane #2 be comfortable?*

Like I was at that age, Jane #2 is a little modest. She is also very petite. Going shopping for such items can be a challenge when you're petite, although I'm guessing bra and bathing suit shopping can be a challenge for women of all sizes and shapes. There was a vast selection of beautiful suits in this store- ready to accommodate all these women of various shapes and sizes. One of the things I noted right away was the good support that the tops gave, something I felt swimsuits in other stores were greatly lacking.

Lesson learned: shop for bathing suits in stores that specialize in quality swimwear and underwear. Your breasts will thank you.

I decided (since I was there) to try on some things myself. I gathered a collection of swimsuits and bras to take to the fitting room. Finding things to potentially fit Jane #2 was a little more challenging, but with Jane #3's help, we were able to find some.

Into the changing room we went, our cubicles side-by-side. I started with bras. *I'm not the only woman who does the bounce test, right?* The bounce test wasn't necessary in my younger days when my breasts were smaller and more dense. But times (and my breasts) have changed, and I needed to ensure that they'd stay well-contained. So bounce, I did.

Jane #3 came in to check on us, and of course bring me more styles and sizes. It was extremely helpful to have a second opinion about size and fit. Where I usually find bra and bathing suit shopping very stressful, this time wasn't.

I noticed that there was not much sound coming from beside me, from Jane #2's stall. This concerned me. Time to do a check-in.

"How are you making out?" I asked.

"Well… I don't know…" she said with great hesitation, and little other information.

I asked if she needed help, but she declined, taking a few more minutes to try to figure it out on her own. She eventually asked me to come into her cubicle. She had concerns about how the bras were fitting. Knowing that Jane #3 would know the fits and options better than I would, I suggested she get her to come help.

My modest daughter didn't jump at that recommendation at first. Her response: "that's just weird. I'll be sitting for family dinner at the table with her, and she's seen me in a bra."

"Well, she's seen me in a bra too, bouncing," I responded. "She'll be picturing both of us. Besides, it will make for a more fun family dinner."

I then added "this is what she does for her job. She's seen

everyone in their bra."

I remember being in that situation when I was young and getting fitted. I'm not sure it's a comfortable experience for anyone that age. But at some point you stop caring.

Jane #2 eventually asked Jane #3 to go in and help her. With great success, they found some bras and underwear that fit well and that she liked. The only thing left was the bathing suits. With my new focus on body positivity, I tried on two-piece bathing suits. I relied on the bounce test again, making sure they'd be well-contained in the event I took up surfboarding. I managed to find (and buy) a top that I could not only surf in, but could also skydive in. No coverage in terms of stomach, thighs and butt being exposed, but… I didn't care.

I wish I had embraced this whole body positivity and acceptance thing a few decades ago.

I was still in the changing room, wearing a somewhat jungle themed two-piece and was feeling rather silly. I began to sing "in the jungle, the mighty jungle, the lion sleeps tonight…" to which I thought would slightly embarrass my daughter.

To my surprise, she chimed in from the next stall and started singing with me. Two goofs in the fitting rooms, singing away. I'm sure the staff and other customers thoroughly enjoyed the entertainment.

We spent a very long time in that store. I think, despite us taking up so much of her time, that Jane #3 still likes us. I guess we will see about that when we're all sitting around the table at our next family dinner, envisioning one another in our bras.

My favourite part about the experience was when my daughter found her bathing suit. She tried on several "safe" ones first. One piece, black…that kind of safe. But just as we were paying for our other items we spotted one that was playful and fun and we had somehow missed. Back into the fitting room we went. When she came out in that cute two-piece, she did a little happy dance.

That was the bathing suit.

SHOPPING: JUSTIFICATIONS AND EXCUSES

After hearing how successful the shopping trip was with my daughter, my niece (who is very close with her) decided that I should take her shopping so she could buy herself a new bathing suit. Let's call her Jane #4.

Jane #4 is a little less modest than my daughter. Probably just the fact that I'm not her mother makes things a bit less awkward for her. We went to the same specialty store that my daughter and I had just gone to. We didn't spend as much time in the store as I had previously, and my soon-to-be sister-in-law was unfortunately not working. Jane #4 was solely there to look for a bathing suit, and I allowed myself to look for bras. (I hadn't actually purchased any the last time.)

I'd been teasing my brother since her birth that I was going to influence her by way of tattoos, piercings, going to bars... Taking her to a lingerie store happened to be pretty fun as well. I discovered that instead of being bummed when I don't like a piece of clothing on myself, I could encourage my young niece to buy it and live vicariously through her. We saw a sweet little bralette that was far too delicate to provide any support to my ba-zongas. But, she tried it on and presto! Super cute.

I, on the other hand, found some practical bras (the same ones

I had bounced around in last time), which I bought. We also both fell in love with (and purchased) some incredibly soft thin lounge/pajama pants. Yes, she did succeed in finding a bathing suit- in fact, the top she purchased was similar to the one I had gotten, with complete worry-free support.

As we were walking through the mall to leave, I was very careful not to look in any stores, despite those window mannequins trying to lure me in. Knowing my birthday was approaching, Jane #4 suggested giving in to the temptation.

"You could buy it for your birthday," she proposed.

Yea..." I said. "But that was my excuse the rest of the month when I bought things."

There are only so many times you can get away with using that excuse. I later realized that I had used quite a number of excuses to justify my purchases in a relatively short period of time. This included, but was probably not limited to:

It's *on sale.*

It's on sale for a good price, which evens out me buying this full price item.

These pretty sandals (which have a name from the retailer) have the same name as our daughter, which is a sign, so I have to buy them.

My boobs overfloweth my other clothes, so I need ones that fit properly.

I'm driving 9 hours and spending 2 days at the children's hospital. I deserve a treat.

This mall is different than the one at home. Let's see what stores are here.

Oh! My favourite store along this long travel route! I only get to go every few years. I'm heading in!

Just because.

That bathing suit I recently wore... I had that before I had kids, 20 years ago. I deserve a new one. (Despite having owned others that I wore in between.)

The angels gave me signs.

My existing clothes are uncomfortable, so I need new ones.

Underwear counts as a necessity item.

It's a wrap dress/shirt. I don't care that I already own several. I have to stock up when I rarely see one.

I am worth it.

This skirt makes my ass look good, I think.

I don't yet own anything in these new seasonal colors or patterns; I should round out my wardrobe.

My daughter will probably wear this too, so I'm not just buying it for me.

Omg this bra is not doing its job. I need a new one; it's an investment.

The number 7.

My partner would think I look pretty in this.

I wouldn't normally wear this, but I'm all pro-body now, so I am going to buy this and wear it with confidence. It's part of my personal growth.

Feel free to borrow any of these if you ever need an excuse to buy something.

I DO NOT WEAR SHORT SHORTS

Do you remember commercials from the 80's for topical hair removal creams?

Let me jog your memory if not: they involved young, attractive, smooth women singing and dancing, flaunting their exposed, long, slim legs.

Smiling, smooth woman: *The Hairy 70's are over… it's time for smooth skin!*

Apply the lotion like so… directly to your leg.

Don't mind the smell- that's the chemicals doing their job!

Leave the product on until the stinging gets intense, but before it gets so unbearable that you start to ugly cry.

Test a spot- has it eaten through the hair yet? If so, gently wipe the product from your leg, being mindful not to wipe off the soft flesh.

Rinse with water for at least 30 minutes, preferably until your well runs dry. If you need to leave the lotion on longer, we suggest having medical professionals on standby.

Provided you haven't passed out from the fumes or pain, don't forget to do your other leg.

Your man is going to love your sexy, smooth legs!

❋ ❋ ❋

There's growing acceptance today for women to stop feeling

pressured to shave, thus leaving their legs, pits and lady bits the way nature intended. Or shave. Whatever we want. The point is, we are now (in 2020) encouraged to decide our own body's hair status because it's our own damn body. Which is pretty cool. Some of us (like me) get lazy with our hair removal. At least I can blame it on feminism, not laziness.

I've been known to tell my partner that my lack of shaving is because I'm seeing how long the hair will grow in.

Nope. Pure laziness.

Seeing as I was born in 1975 and was slow to develop (and blonde), I didn't worry much about hair on my legs in the 80's. I also didn't have to worry too much about chub on my legs while wearing short shorts. In fact, a lot of women didn't worry. There was little reason to. The 80's was a time when fast food and convenience items were only beginning to get popular. Junk was a treat, not a part of our everyday lives. Sometimes when I watch movies from a few decades ago, I'm in awe of just how sleek people were, seemingly without effort. *Was there a shortage of food??!?*

I'm left with pangs of both sadness and envy.

❦ ❦ ❦

I've been a skirt and dress wearer the past few years, particularly in the summer. I occasionally wear skirts and dresses in cold months as well, provided I can keep my legs and feet warm. Skirts and dresses are comfy. They aren't tight on the thighs, or bum. And if you can find ones that wrap or tie, you can also avoid having any waistbands digging uncomfortably into your belly. With a dress, one can also avoid the muffin-top, over-floweth issue... you know what I'm talking about ladies.

There's no need to think about your thighs when you're wearing a skirt that's to your knees or longer. I've acquired quite a collection of long skirts. The downside though, is that although they're comfortable and flowy, long skirts trap heat underneath. This is problematic when it's July, you've underestimated the heat, and you don't have anything else to change into. You can't roll up a skirt like a pant leg. Although in a pinch of desperation, you can use a hair elastic to tie a skirt up in a ridiculous looking way.

How nuns ever wore those black floor-length habits is beyond me.

If you have daughters, you probably know how hard it is to find shorts that attempt to adhere to a school dress code. Well, I don't have any dress code to dictate my shorts length, but I still don't care to have my ass cheeks hanging out for all to see. Not that there's anything wrong with butt cheeks necessarily, but publicly showing them is not really my thing.

On a daily basis though I'd see women out and about in their shorts, seemingly oblivious to showing their cellulite to the world. I'd watch them with great curiosity. If they don't care, why should I? So, with my newfound, somewhat forced acceptance of my body as it is, I decided it was time to buy some shorts, even if they were a bit shorter than I had previously been comfortable with.

And so I did buy some shorts, as chronicled in my shopping chapter.

※ ※ ※

On one particular day, I knew I was dressing not only for the heat, but also for two appointments. Dressing for appointments in the summer is difficult; you don't know which places will have soul-piercing air conditioning, and which should have a warning sign on the door that says "Heat warning. Enter at your own risk." There's also the *inside... outside... in the car... in a (possibly?) air-conditioned store... in the car... outside again... and repeat* thing.

I'm guessing maybe it's a preview for hormonal hot flashes. Can't wait.

Because I spend so much of my time at home in my pajamas, I usually try to make myself look presentable when going out for things such as appointments. But even more of an incentive was the fact that it was our anniversary, and my partner and I were planning on having dinner together afterwards. I wanted to decrease any chance that he would have second thoughts about me during the dinner, which is why I chose to put in some effort.

In preparation for my big outing, I spent time on my makeup, and was quite satisfied with the end result. My hair was washed and brushed. My legs and armpits were actually shaved.

I was a tad excited to put on the brand spankin' new shorts that I had recently purchased. They were a different color and style than anything I had previously owned.

And, these dressy shorts had nice POCKETS.

I did a rear check for underwear lines (which led to a quick underwear change), but I refrained from scrutinizing my legs or their cellulite. Those shorts were cute. I was totally feeling them. I was gonna strut myself to those appointments and dinner and not care. But then I hit a brief snag.

The shorts were a bit awkward to pair with anything because of the colors and also the style. I didn't have any white shirts that tucked in well. Then I remembered- I had just bought that simple white shirt that was waist length.

I paired the new white shirt with the shorts and got ready to leave. However, I made the mistake of giving myself one last look-over. *What the hell was that??!!??*

I made an interesting discovery. Not only do I put on weight on my booty and boobs, but also on my back. My back. *What?!?* I had back fat. In order for me to have the freakin' bra tight enough to hold up my freakin' aging boobs, it was cutting into my flesh and bulging around the bottom strap.

I know, this shouldn't surprise me. It's just not something I had ever dealt with before. The thin shirt fabric wasn't helping, as it was accentuating the bulging. So, I changed into a thicker shirt. I could still see it. I changed to another bra, even daring to adjust to a looser hook than usual. The bra still embraced my back fat.

There was a time when this new discovery would have sincerely devastated me. A time when I would have tried on another 72 shirts, only to find that I was still unhappy plus had a huge mound of clothes on my floor. But, I refuse to go there to that place. I spent too much time there. I've moved forward.

In defiance, I spun around and left our bedroom. The voice in my head, to no one in particular: *Let 'em look. We women don't put on weight and fill out our bosom without a little back fat too. Deal with it...*

With my look complete and without question, I confidently walked out to the kitchen to collect my daughter to go to our appointment. My partner saw me and said "those shorts look really nice on you," and then embraced me and looked into my eyes. He didn't see the back fat. He didn't feel the back fat. He just saw and felt *me*.

❊ ❊ ❊

Short shorts were popular with men (ON MEN) at one time (I believe in the 70's?), but not so much anymore. Have men developed better fashion sense than women? Or do they avoid short shorts because they fear something breaking loose and hanging below their hem line?

We may never know.

❊ ❊ ❊

Imagine my surprise when my daughter came to me wanting to remove the hair from her legs for the first time.

"Can we get some of that cream?" she asked.

"The cream you put on your legs that eats through the hair?" I said.

"Yes," she responded.

I pushed on. "The cream that makes your nostrils burn? Did

you read what I wrote about that?"

She looked confused. "No…?"

"Hmm… that's weird that you're asking, because I recently wrote about that. They still make that stuff?" I asked, surprised.

"I'm afraid of razors," she explained further. "I want to try the cream instead."

Part of me was a bit sad that my youngest had crossed over into the wanting to remove her leg hair phase. I was also sceptical about the product and its safety, but due to her fear of razor blades I thought I would let her try it. I had expected the trial to go down *with* incident, which I would then follow with a lesson on how to use a razor.

I was getting ready and didn't have the time at that moment, so her stepfather took her to the pharmacy to choose and purchase the product. Of course, I thought this father/daughter moment was super cute.

She did a patch test to check for any sensitivities. The result was negative. She was ready to do an entire leg.

That night, she closed herself into the bathroom and trialed the product before her shower. We all waited with worried anticipation, from the comfort of the living room, where we were chilling with Netflix.

"Oh no! That stuff is terrible," said one of the girls.

"Make sure you turn the fan on!" her sister piped.

I was already dreading the migraine I was expecting soon from the fumes.

We wondered how long it would be before we'd have to go in and rescue her from the strong chemicals. But, the chemical smell never did reach us. She eventually called me into the bathroom to see the result.

The result?? I couldn't even smell the stuff, so I couldn't believe there was an actual result. I picked up the bottle, took off the cover and smelled it. It smelled, almost… pleasant. And not at all strong. Sometime in the last 15 years they must have changed the formula and made it 5,000,000 times more improved.

I must say, it worked quite well. We had been worried about her skin initially because she's had eczema her entire life, including on her legs. The hair removal product seemed to work as a bit of an exfoliant for her too. It was the first time in her life that she'd had really smooth legs, which was a big deal. She was excited. I was excited for her. Now I'm wondering if they sell it in a family size, since we're all going to want to use it as our go-to hair removal method.

RAISING DAUGHTERS

Having daughters was something that both excited me and filled me with fear. On one hand, I felt I had great wisdom to share that could help influence other young women to be confident and prepared. On the other hand, I was terrified that my daughters would face challenges similar to mine. I wanted to help them avoid that at all costs.

I tried to impart body positivity on my girls from the beginning. I was determined to provide them with only a positive role model – the most healthy version of myself. This was easier said than done. I forced myself to exude confidence in my own skin. It definitely began as a "fake it" situation.

If you were to ask my daughters today, they'd likely tell you they saw too much of their mother puttering around the house in her bra and underwear. They'd probably tell you they'd seen enough of my naked boobs and ass toddling from the bedroom to the bathroom, and back again. But I would hazard a guess that they would also tell you that they had no idea of my personal struggles with body image. I certainly didn't discuss my body in any kind of shameful manner.

When other mothers would complain about their bellies or their weight or how poorly their clothes fit, I did not. I was acutely aware that girls are constantly bombarded with messages from media of unachievable body standards and body dissatisfaction. They didn't need to hear that in the home from their mother as well.

I was the mom who didn't have an issue with my girls seeing

a woman's naked body, as long as it wasn't sexualized. I embraced movements like #freethenipple. I wanted my daughters to see what women looked like- different types of women- with different sized and shaped breasts, different everything. I had grown up in an age before the internet. I didn't have access to photos of women and what they looked like nude, and when I did (such as finding that "dirty" magazine in the woods) I would study the photos, curious because I had nothing else to compare myself to. *Did I look like that?* Of course, you can imagine the body type that these women had; there wasn't much diversity in those magazines. I wanted different for my daughters.

I spoke with my girls a lot about a healthy body rather than a healthy weight. It was never about weight. Their father and I had been very tiny children, and I knew our children were likely destined to be petite, for awhile anyway. Sometimes it was unavoidable to not talk about their size, because they were so small compared to their peers. When it came to food, I emphasized that we eat for nutrition, and we should eat the healthy things our body needs for fuel. Provided we did this, having treats was ok in moderation. We didn't discuss trying to control one's weight. My philosophy was that one's body would settle to where it was naturally meant to be, if we fuelled it as best we could. And that was that.

I didn't weigh the girls after they were infants. They were occasionally weighed by doctors, which was helpful in dosing them with ibuprophen or other medication when they needed it. (They were so small that we always had to dose them on the low end, by weight, not age.)

Despite all my previous issues, I managed to pull off the impossible: I faked body confidence for 16 years.

What I didn't expect was that in faking it for them, it slowly changed the way I felt about myself and my own body. I actually became more confident and at peace with my body after having kids than I had been when I was young, before having children.

I had always been very honest with my children. I had always talked about difficult things without shame, and wanted them to have the confidence to do the same. But, I hadn't discussed my younger struggles with them. In a way I was scared to; I feared putting ideas into their heads. I know this is completely ridiculous- that somehow it would influence them into going down that same ugly road. But, that's what fear does- it makes us think irrationally. So, I had been transparent with most other things in my life, including having challenges with depression and anxiety, but I purposefully kept this part of myself and my past from them.

I always assumed that one day I would reveal this when the girls were older. I wanted to be able to own this as part of who I was- who I am- without there being shame in it. But, I did still feel shame.

When my daughter was a teenager, I broached this subject with her. She seemed surprised by the new information. Even more surprisingly, I found the conversation to be very awkward. It was still hard for me to admit that this had been my experience. Somehow, I still blamed myself.

I didn't realize that being in this role (a mother to daughters) would be so healing to me in my own recovery. I have developed an indescribable survival instinct and resiliency that I'm certain I could not have developed without my children.

※ ※ ※

When my daughters were young, I had the idea that something might happen to me before I had the chance to teach them all my womanly knowledge. So, I started writing them letters (which I filed away) so they'd have a means to access my motherly advice should I have an early demise.

I got behind writing those letters. When I say "behind", I mean probably 13 or so years behind. Lucky for them I didn't get hit by a bus, so I've been around to share some of my invaluable life experience directly. I failed at letters, but I succeeded in so many other ways.

I guess in a way this book is my collection of letters to my daughters. To other daughters. To sons. To myself.

My love story.

❋ ❋ ❋

Upon not being able to find my eyebrow liner & brush, I addressed our 3 teenage daughters.

"Has anyone taken my eyebrow liner? It's missing."

13 year old: "what color is it?"

Me: "um... my eyebrow color."

17 year old ignores conversation.

13 year old: "where was it?"

Me: "uh... with all the rest of my makeup in the bedroom."

14 year old: "How long haven't you been able to find it? If it's only been a few days... (trails off)...but if it's been like a few months, *that* could be me."

❋ ❋ ❋

Many months later... discovered why the 17 year old was pretending to ignore the conversation...

LEGS, PITS AND LADY BITS

I didn't feel this book would be complete without a "lady bits" chapter.

I had penned several potential cheeky titles for this chapter, but I (somewhat) reluctantly discarded them. I was fearful that my children wouldn't speak with me again if I used any of them.

❉ ❉ ❉

We females are at a significant disadvantage when it comes to getting to know and understand our genitalia. Male genitals are inescapable, flopping around or at attention front and center, whereas ours are tucked away out of our view. Unless we use a mirror, we never get a good look at what's actually down there, which is unfathomable to men since they are so undeniably familiar with their penises. As such, there are women who go through their entire life without ever looking at their own vagina. Like, ever.

My apologies- vulva. "Vagina" refers to the canal, while vulva refers to the other parts that make up the female genital area, the external parts.

You'd think that an area of our bodies that is important for many reasons would be something we'd be curious about and naturally become familiar with. But, the vulva is arguably one of the most oppressed things known to humankind. We've been discouraged to show it, to touch it, to enjoy it. We've been taught that it can be dirty. Generations of women were encouraged to make their nether regions smell like delicate flowers, with the help of commercial "cleansing" products. There has been a great wall of shame built up around the vulva- a wall that only one's husband was allowed to break through for quite some time.

Things are changing. Although there are still improvements to be made, sex education has evolved. Our youth are being taught the proper physiology, although school curriculum (in our area anyway), has thus far neglected to acknowledge female sexual pleasure. But even though they're taught the parts, it's by way of a colorless, basic line drawing. This type of drawing doesn't really depict a true vulva, and certainly doesn't show the way in which vulvas look different from person to person.

Unless she takes a hand mirror and looks- and is comfortable in doing so- a female can't really get to know her *down there*.

There's little wonder that so many ask… *am I normal?*

When you're growing up and your body is changing it can be a very insecure time. We want confirmation that our parts are normal. The truth that we are so infrequently told is that they can all look very different, so *there is no one normal vulva.*

I always wanted my daughters to know that genitalia, like breasts, can look very different and change throughout one's life, which is very "normal". And that they vary from person to person, which is also "normal." Yes, I was that mom who was like "look at all these different types of breasts!" which they didn't really enjoy. They enjoyed it even less when I wanted to show them vaginas.

I'm surprised my children still talk to me.

If you have not seen the sculpture by artist Jamie McCartney called The Great Wall of Vaginas, I would highly recommend Googling it. He made plaster castings of 400 different vaginas, and then made the collection into a wall sculpture. It is oddly mesmerizing. There are so many similarities yet differences. Because it's made as a plaster sculpture rather than photos of skin, it's a bit less intimidating to get all up in there to view closely, for those of us who are a little faint of heart. There is an unexpected great beauty in a wall of plastered vaginas.

In writing this, I needed to look up the artist's name online. As I was considering this piece again, I said aloud "I really do find The Great Wall of Vaginas fascinating."

To which my partner replied "you're looking at The Great Wall of Vaginas again??"

Chuckling, I said "yes."

"Honey... *AGAIN??*"

Yes.

Rhetorical question?

The same artist also made a penis wall sculpture, also viewable online. I find the penises all sticking out like that to be quite amusing.

It would make a really freakin' awesome hat rack.

SCALES MEASURE WEIGHT, NOT HAPPINESS

I don't "diet" (verb). But I have tried a diet (noun). The low FODmap diet, that is. If you're not familiar, the low FODmap diet is what you adopt when you've been waiting for 2 years for a gastroenterologist and you're so beyond desperate that you willingly give up eating pretty much everything that you love. I won't get into all the medical specifics, but the purpose is to find your digestive system's trigger foods, eliminate them, and get your system working properly again. At that point, you can test to see which foods cause issues as you add them back into your diet individually.

Following the FODmap diet was very difficult for me. Garlic and onions apparently can be significant gastric triggers and should be avoided at all costs, especially during the elimination period. But, eliminating garlic and onions also eliminated some of my instinctive will to live, which seemed a tad counterproductive.

However, becoming more aware of gastric triggers was very helpful in me having some control over pain and bloating. So, I did have some success overall. My family doctor also prescribed a medication that drastically improved my quality of life.

The result? I felt better. Not perfect, but significantly better.

My children were happy that I was able to engage with them again, but they soon got tired of me announcing every bowel movement I had, like I was a 2 year old potty training. I did suggest a sticker chart with a reward, but they didn't appease my request.

So you see, I'm not just figuratively full of shit, but also literally full of shit.

Now you're asking... *why the heck is this relevant?*

It was SO difficult for me not to weigh myself after each good bowel movement. I was convinced that I would weigh-in significantly lighter after doing so. *I'm not the only one who does this, right?* I hadn't implemented the FODmap diet to lose weight, but I had decided that it would've been a nice side effect. However, the Guts Gods didn't bless me with a 15 lb weight loss. My flatter belly was heavenly though.

※ ※ ※

There was a time when I didn't own a scale. I'm not sure when or how one snuck back into the house, but it did. Not wanting it to be a focal point, I've kept it "hidden" in the bedroom, not in the bathroom. I was hoping that by not having it in sight, the children would be less tempted to follow their weight. Usually the kids didn't know their weight at any given time, so I believe my plan worked. They also didn't seem to care what it was.

When I'm at other people's houses and I see a bathroom scale, I can't help but get on it. I'm driven by compulsion. Do I weigh significantly different on their scale? I wonder if they hear me getting on it. I'm careful to be very quiet, because a bathroom scale makes that tell-tale metal sound on the floor.

I feel like it's a weird thing to weigh yourself on someone else's bathroom scale. I wonder how many other people do the same thing.

In my later years, I vowed not to be controlled by a scale and the numbers on it. It became a bit hard to ignore when I outgrew my clothes. It wasn't my weight though that became my prison- it was my clothing. I didn't want to let go of clothes that I liked, or admit that they didn't fit properly anymore. So, I'd wear them and be uncomfortable and at times even pained. What had once been a flattering outfit started to not contain me; I'd spill out of my top, and overflow out of my jeans. Like many other women, I was so happy to be back into pre-children jeans or a size that I could wear before, that I refused to admit that cramming myself in didn't do me any favors.

Sometimes denial is a beautiful thing. But, not in that case.

There was a time when I'd get very hung up on clothing sizes. With age, I've come to understand the inconsistency with sizes. Manufacturers seem to have their own sizing at times. The way a garment fits can depend much on the person's frame than the number on the tag. Sometimes the sizes seem random- like they're pulling them out of a hat. Sometimes they seem so completely unrealistic that it's almost comical *(how can I be a large in this shirt??)*

I guess there was a time, around my teenage years, that my peers shared their clothing sizes with one another. At that time, I felt like I had a certain standard to maintain. But one day as an adult it dawned on me- no one asks what size is on my clothing tags. Eventually I also realized that when I stopped trying to cram myself into a certain size and wear clothing that fit my body better, it looked better. And I felt better both physically and emotionally.

※ ※ ※

On one occasion I was wearing new shorts I had just bought. They were bigger in size than what I had been wearing, but fit my body better. I felt good in the outfit. I left our bedroom, and walked by my partner, as he was taking a bite out of an apple. He called me over.

"You're sexy," he said.

He was looking deep into my eyes as he said it. It wasn't about the clothing, not directly anyway. But, I was exuding confidence in the clothing and feeling better about myself. That's what he was picking up on.

I packed up all that smaller clothing that I had been trying to cram myself into.

SOCIAL MEDIA SPIES AND SOCIAL MEDIA SIZE

If I see another company try to sell me their "period panty" on my social media feed, I will lose it. I have no desire to sit around in bloody underwear all day.

Curse you Facebook for insisting we register with our age, gender and relationship status!

I hate the targeted ads. When I'm having a lazy Saturday afternoon perusing the Internet with no given purpose I don't want all that crap cluttering up my social media feed.

On one recent lazy Saturday afternoon, one of these ads featured a slim young woman, with very round, perky breasts. She looked a little like Barbie. I'm quite certain they weren't her natural breasts. It didn't look as if they were going to move too far, if at all.

The ad was for a product that markets itself to be a strapless bra, claiming to lift one's breasts. The sticky little thing adheres to your breast, you pull it up, you stick it down- presto!! Your boobs are somewhere up around your chin.

I was baffled by the company's choice of model. I took a screenshot and sent it to my friend with the caption "does it look like she needs a breast lift??? %^#@#@$#!!! No wonder women are so hard on their bodies." Of course, she agreed with me.

With curiosity, I took time to go through more ads. Some were there because clearly they've been spying on me with their adware and special cookies. No, not those kind of special cookies. The computer-y kind of creepy, *spying* cookies. I recognized this right away because it was showing me shopping sites I had previously visited and particular clothing that had caught my eye. They were trying to lure me back.

However, I have NOT been looking for period underwear or breast lift products.

This led me to wonder what shows up in the feeds of men my age. My guy wasn't there at the time of this particular Saturday reflection, so rather than ask him any burning questions about manly middle-aged advertisements, I went back to looking at the sticky breast-lifter ads.

My curiosity got the best of me, and I went to the reviews to read more, like the savvy online shopper that I am. I quickly found out that reading reviews for breast products is much more entertaining than reading reviews for a toaster.

There were only 8 reviews on this particular website, which is not much considering how many breasts are out there in the world that are longing to be lifted. All the reviews were good and each happy customer had posted a picture of their cleavage. (Apparently I'm not the only woman who gets excited about anything that makes my breasts look better.)

The photos were a nice addition. They *definitely* made it more interesting than reading reviews for a toaster.

To my surprise, the website said you could reuse the boob stickies several times. It didn't specify how many times "several" was. I began to daydream about a world in which my breasts were glamorous.

I'm on my way to the Oscars, wearing a slightly provocative but classy gown. I want to look my very best tonight because I'm up for an award. Like the other female Oscar-goers, I feel the pressure to have my breasts closer to my chin than my navel. Thus, I wear a pair of sticky boob-lifters. I hadn't purchased a new set as I had blown my budget on a beautiful pair of diamond-encrusted shoes for that night. The boob-lifter package had said "several wears" so there was no need to waste money on another set.

I arrive in the limo on time, and make it through the pre-awards photo shoots with dignity and grace. An hour later, I wait in my chair a tad nervous. The room is hot and I start to sweat, more because of the heat than nerves. I praise myself for buying a dress that is well ventilated in front and back, and for remembering to wear extra deodorant, so I didn't stink out Ryan Reynolds, who is sitting beside me. No, he isn't there as my date. (I'm a happily engaged woman!) Ryan and I chat about our new film roles, and that steamy sex scene we filmed together last fall.

They call out the names of the nominees. And the winner is... My name gets called and applause fills the room, I won! OMG, I won!!! Ryan gives me a congratulatory kiss on the mouth, with a bit of tongue. The next 40 seconds is a blur as I make my way through the maze of people, make my way to the stage and approach the podium to accept my award. I feel... ... the sticky on my left breast is sliding. SPLAT!! It lands on the podium. My right breast is still up, ready for a night of post awards partying. But my spirits are as deflated at that point as my left breast.

As I've alluded to, I don't have a lot of faith in this product for me. I also feel as though it would flatten my breasts, rather than lift them. The woman in the advertisement had clearly not breastfed several children.

※ ※ ※

I have to give credit to some women's retailers. They FINALLY started listening to women about what we want to see. In recent days, there has been a movement to include women of all shapes and sizes to model underwear and other clothing. These women are more relatable to the majority of us. They show "life experience" on their bodies: love handles, extra skin from losing weight, cellulite, stretch marks, wrinkles, flatter or smaller breasts. Feedback from consumers has been very positive.

Sometimes I'll see a piece of clothing on someone with a rockin' body and am drawn to it. But, *if the body of the woman isn't relatable to my own, how am I supposed to believe it will look on my own body?*

There was once an online store that I loved and followed for many years. Their clothes were a tad expensive, so that alone kept me from making any impulse buys. But, I would often save items from that store in my favourites. Of course, they would pop up from time to time, and I'd stare longingly at the pictures.

I'm convinced that the retailer was trying to sell me the body, not the clothes. It appeared that they used only the one model, consistently. Her face was never shown. Her body was the definition of sexy. Cur-VY. A tiny, tiny waist. Very large breasts. Curvy hips, and a beautiful bum. No, not a bum. An ass. She probably gets followed through the mall by... well, everyone. The clothes were always very tight fitting. The tops were low-cut and tight... the pants were tight... Nothing was left to the imagination. You catch my drift.

Obviously they did a great job selling me on her body.

However, I didn't have that body. What would those clothes look like on me? Yes, I had curves, but I wasn't built like her. I struggled to understand which size would fit me properly, if at all.

What size was she even wearing? Some women with large breasts are petite but can't fit into a small or medium size. I wasn't able to make a connection between her and I, to picture how the clothing would look on someone like me. Due to the price of the items and suspecting how difficult it would have been to make a return, I don't think I ever did purchase anything from them.

Many retailers in the past 2 years are using photos of models that are much less edited, which is why we can see stretch marks on bellies and cellulite on thighs. Don't get me wrong- I know this isn't completely for the Consumer's benefit. Their main goal is still to make money, not to make bold social statements and to challenge worldviews. Still, it's been very refreshing to see, and to witness the responses that people are having to the change. It's a heck of a lot more nourishing for the soul to read comments about embracing body positivity than the plethora of online negativity.

I'm noticing that my own views have even evolved, as I've been exposed to women of all shapes and sizes wearing all kinds of clothing. Thinking about leggings for instance- there was once the general belief that a woman needed to have a certain body type to wear them. As time passed, more and more companies started producing plus-sized leggings, and advertisements began including models that are much larger than a size 2.

I love seeing women saying *this is my body, this is what I want to wear on it, and screw you if you don't like it.*

I consider myself to be a pretty open and accepting person. But, I admit (with a bit of embarrassment) I've had fleeting thoughts about what someone should wear. Well, more like what they perhaps should *not* wear. Not too long ago I drove past a young woman who was wearing a tight crop top and very tight leggings. She was showing her middle and was quite overweight. The thought that there might be something more flattering for her to wear popped into my head.

As soon as I caught myself thinking that way, I redirected. My mindset shifted. I realized how confident this young woman was, which was admirable. I wish I had had that confidence when I was her age, to dress the way I wanted. I wish I had been less inhibited by my own insecurities.

Without even realizing it, we often have expectations of what people should or shouldn't wear, simply based on their body type. Think about these statements:

You should dress to hide your "problem areas."
She could wear a garbage bag and still look good.
Can she pull off that crop top?

Plus sized women shouldn't wear stripes.

These are good bathing suit styles for your body type (curvy, short, hourglass, square).

We are bombarded with messages about how we are expected to present our bodies in clothing. Think of the freedom we'd have if we all were free to wear whatever the heck we wanted to, without unneeded judgement.

How to Get a Bikini Body... if you're a woman, you've been exposed to this recycled magazine topic probably a hundred or more times throughout your life. I don't even read the magazine articles, yet there they are- staring me in the face every time I'm standing in line, waiting to put through my grocery order.

You look over and see a magazine with a scantily clad woman on the front, boasting the headline Get a Bikini Body in time for Summer or How I Lost 20 lbs in One Month Eating Only Cardboard. Do you:

1. Open the magazine and skim it quickly, to try to figure out what kind of cardboard you should be eating to get that bikini body.

2. Bypass that article and check out whatever (likely fabricated) drama is going on with the royal family that week.

3. Make small talk with the woman standing behind you. You realize she has a basket full of ice cream and condoms and try (awkwardly) to keep your gaze from wandering to her basket. You want to ask if she's just started a bad breakup, acting out sexually and sobbing into buckets of ice cream.

4. Turn your back to the magazines, but now you're facing the chocolate bars. The temptation is too great. If this is the option you choose, toss a few bars into the woman's basket behind you, because she probably needs some too.

My favourite sentiment when it comes to how to get a bikini body... "Put on a bikini. Go to the beach."

The point being, *any* body is a bikini body.

The most powerful bathing suit testimonials come from mothers who eventually *get it*. They were women who once didn't participate in activities with their kids, because they were too ashamed to put on a bathing suit. Then they realize they've been missing out on all the experiences and making memories with their children, and they put on that damn bathing suit and enjoy themselves.

※ ※ ※

One of the reasons I'm drawn to social media is because it's such a powerful tool for staying connected. What I dislike about it is the superficiality and cruelty from commenters. It's upsetting that so many people are purposefully hurtful with one another. I generally try to avoid comments that I expect will be negative and unhealthy to read.

I finally bit the bullet and joined Instagram about a year ago. From what I've seen, Instagram seems to be most used by younger generations, not women in their 40's. Being a photo-sharing platform, there's a lot of posting of "selfies" and people seeking validation for the way they look. Don't get me wrong- I enjoy getting likes on a flattering photo of myself. But platforms like Instagram feed into the addictive need to constantly validate one's appearance by way of input from others.

What I do like about Instagram is the new(er) online movement that focuses on body acceptance and positivity. I avoid messages that I may have been more attracted to in my younger days (promoting slim figures, weight loss); I gravitate to those that focus on positive self-talk and promote a healthier body image.

Whoever coined the term Social Media Influencer hit the nail on the head. They undoubtedly heavily influence their followers, and they're now pulling in big bucks when it comes to consumer goods. People of all ages run to purchase the clothing, makeup and other products that their favourite influencers use and promote.

I follow a woman on Instagram who struggled with accepting herself in her younger years and still does at times today. I can relate to her story of being broken. Of finding and redefining herself. Of finding deep, true love with a man who became her second husband. She is one of the most authentic people that I've come across on social media, and with that genuineness she has built a significant following.

Of course, one of the most important parts of her accepting herself has been finally appreciating her physical body.

In one of her posts, she talks about "showing up." It ties in with my earlier sentiment about worrying too much about what you look like and then missing out on enjoying life with loved ones. She encourages people to "show up", without diminishing how difficult it can be. She shares that although difficult at first, it gets easier, and it's worth it.

This really resonates with me. I've been in that position where I've been so uncomfortable with my body that it's kept me from enjoying myself. So not too long ago, I made the conscious decision not to let a bathing suit or anything else keep me from doing what I'd like to do.

Awhile back my partner and I planned an overnight trip at a nice hotel, just the two of us. The hotel had a large indoor pool, a hot tub and a waterslide. I knew that I was *not* going to let my insecurities keep me from enjoying that hot tub, as my sore body was longing to be soaked. I was "showing up." He knew what I meant when I said this. Interestingly, when I told my teenage daughter "I'm showing up", she suspected some kind of inappropriate idea was brewing in my head, and that I was going to act on it.

"I don't want to know," she said.

I assured her that it was all positive and that I'd explain at a later point.

By saying it aloud, I had committed myself. I wasn't going to miss out. I wasn't going to worry about my stomach (in a two piece bathing suit). I wasn't going to worry about my thighs or butt. I was going to show up. And importantly, have fun.

To be completely transparent, I did worry a tad about my bathing suit top bursting open, but with good reason. The clasp on the back had broken, and so I did what any woman does when she wants to wear a broken bathing suit top: I sewed it together with dental floss. The fact that my breasts were now far bigger than they were when I used to wear the top also made me a bit concerned, but I pushed on.

Well, we got to the indoor pool area, and there was an enormous waterslide there. I am deathly afraid of heights. And claustrophobic. And this very high waterslide was also completely enclosed, twisting and turning all the way down. But, I had gotten it into my head that I was "showing up" for this waterslide.

%&$#!

(I don't know why I do these kinds of things to myself.)

I had already committed, so I felt like I had to go through with it. If I had backed out, the only witness would have been my partner. In all fairness to him, he would never push me toward doing something I couldn't do. But he is an encourager, and will challenge me to test my perceived limits. I didn't need to prove anything to him; I wanted to prove it to myself.

I watched a few teenage boys throw themselves down the slide, feeling like if I studied what they were doing that it would somehow help me. They were flying out of the bottom of that thing.

I finally mustered up the guts to ask "how was it?"

"Kind of scary, but fun," one said.

"It makes your stomach flip," said the other.

They went down a few times, so clearly it wasn't too terrible. Maybe.

My partner went down. He said it was a little scary, but really fun and worth it. I could see the rush of excitement in his smile.

I climbed the staircase, choosing to lose count of how many stairs I had to climb. I stood at the top, frozen in fear. I let others who had climbed up after me go ahead of me.

While I stood frozen, a little girl came up and shrieked "yea! This is so much fun!!" and tossed herself down the slide.

%&$#!

Now I really had to do it.

I was envious of the girl's confidence and lack of fear. I stood at the top of the slide. I laid down, still holding on. I prayed that my top wouldn't bust open, leaving me bare-chested at the bottom, traumatizing anyone.

My partner told me to let go, count to 5 slowly and I'd be safely down at the bottom.

I let go. In terror, I counted, but there was no counting slowly. I counted at record speed as I sped down that slide, taking those winding turns like I was luging in the winter Olympics. I reached the number 18 at about the halfway point. When I emerged from the bottom I was certain I had swallowed half the pool. My stomach had definitely flipped. But, my top was still on. I decided to challenge the dental floss once more and went down again, this time holding my nose. And yes, I still counted like my life depended on it.

Even though this was out of my comfort zone for a few reasons, I'm so glad I pushed myself. There were many laughs and a great memory created. I'm proud to say, I showed up.

※ ※ ※

Ableism is another "ism" that (specifically in regards to sexuality) is prevalent throughout social media.

Sadly, many have bought into the notion that those who have disabilities are not sexual beings. Some view those adults with developmental and/or physical disabilities as more childlike and thus not "allowed" to express this side.

Unfortunately, many view a disabled body as broken, and not desirable. I love seeing people who actively challenge this, as do a few individuals that I follow. One particular person is a very smart, well-spoken young 20 something woman. I'm unsure of her specific diagnosis (if she indeed has one), as it was never something I felt of relevance. I enjoy her posts because of the way she challenges ableist views. I even appreciate when she gets frustrated and when that frustration comes through. I sometimes sense the slight snarkiness that I'd expect from any 20 something year old who feels continuously oppressed and bold enough to give voice to it.

She often posts photos of herself that you'd see of other young Instagram social influencers: a little on the scantily clad side, even what we would consider to be seductively posed. The difference is, her body isn't quite what we usually see when we look at the female figure, and it makes some people uncomfortable.

The maddening thing is, her photos are often flagged as inappropriate and removed. Other (able-bodied) young women post similar "sexy" photos on a regular basis, even more provocative and less covered than hers. And yet, they remain unflagged online. I've read the furthering frustration she feels when this happens. It makes me angry for her. I get the sense that she doesn't want to feel like she has to be an advocate- that she just wants to feel like she can live her life and have the same opportunities as her peers- that she just wants to be able to post a skimpy bikini picture and have the right to do so while feeling safe and respected.

I appreciate the message that this young woman has helped me and so many others see. No, her body isn't quite what we usually see when we look at the female figure- but I like that. All bodies can be beautiful and attractive.

HOW DO MY JIBBIES SMELL?

After meeting my partner's friend, I was curious to know his first impression of me.

"Did he say anything about me?" I queried. Did he think I seemed nice... smart... we're a well-suited couple...

He hesitated, then said "he thought you had big tits."

Really?

REALLY??

How flattering. I was reduced to "tits."

Now, in this person's defense, I've since gotten to know him and he's a really good guy. But I was taken aback by this response, especially since my partner himself is not someone to objectify a woman like this. An opposites attract kind of friendship?

Truth be told, my surprise was less about the fact that he said that, and more about the fact he had said that about *me. That's how others see me? As having big breasts?*

When did this happen? Is there an imaginary sizing line you cross... from small-ish to moderate to large breasts? When did I cross that line?

I have always disliked the word tits. Many, many years ago (like 24), when I was younger and I'd hear a male refer to someone's large breasts as "tits", I would engage in a heated argument in which I would passionately disagree with the use of that word. To be completely transparent, most times I was under the influence of alcohol, which only added to my feistiness.

In my mind, "tits" sounds small. I've always felt like the term used should best reflect the breast size, and "tits" doesn't seem to fit if the breasts fit into a moderate to large category.

This added to my confusion when his friend said I had big tits.

Recently (but certainly not the first time), my partner and I had a conversation about breast size terminology. Luckily in this day and age, we can rely on reputable medical resources, such as Dr. Google. And also our slang anatomy expert, Urban Dictionary.

From what I've read to date, I'm fairly certain that most contributors to Urban Dictionary are men. Since men consider themselves to be breast experts, I feel their input here is relevant.

As of the entry in 2003 (a little dated, I know), there is a Breast Scale from 1 to 10, in terms of size. (Not to be confused with shape, because there are many different breast shapes.) This entry ranks breasts from very small to very large:

1. flat
2. fried eggs
3. titties
4. tits
5. jibbies
6. boobs
7. broobs
8. breasts
9. jugs
10. melons

by Who's huw, November 06, 2003

(I'm assuming that's *Doctor* Who's Huw.)

Since we discovered this scale, these terms have entered many a conversation in our home. Neither of us had heard of broobs or jibbies prior to this point. Perhaps there is a geographical influence on the terminology that we aren't aware of, like maybe jibbies is only used on the west coast.

Is a broob a bro-boob? (man boob?)

We still have no idea, but we did manage to incorporate the terms "jibbies" and "broobs" into our usual breast dialogue, so perhaps they'll catch on in our area.

Fried eggs… I had never heard of this. My partner had. I guess it makes a little sense, therefore, I didn't question the validity of this one.

While we generally agreed on the rest of the names on the list, we were surprised by some obvious omissions. Cannons and tatas were not included. Perhaps they weren't popular terms in 2003.

The ratings on the scale didn't seem to mirror what we had been led to expect. On one hand, I was able to state with some confidence that tits (and titties) would place at the lower end of the scale, which I had been adamantly (sometimes drunkenly) arguing about for nearly 25 years. The unfamiliar jibbies and broobs terms were throwing us off in regards to sizing. We also couldn't agree on which was bigger- melons, jugs or (our addition to the scale) cannons.

As with most things biological, I'm sure someday a team of specialists will clearly classify breast size (if they haven't already). Until then, we can only speculate.

❋ ❋ ❋

Like every typical evening, I was nuzzled into my partner's armpit. And like every other time, I expressed my sleepiness and my contentment with a "mmmm…"

But this was not a typical evening.

My "mmmm…" was met with "I don't know why you like my stinky armpit."

I launched into a description about why I liked this particular spot of his to nuzzle into. "It's soft right there (running my fingers up the side of his chest)… then your armpit hair holds your smell. It's my comfort."

I could not have anticipated what would happen next.

"Well," he said. "I kind of understand. Your boobs are the same way."

"Your comfort?" I asked, not surprised at this point. Of course the pillowy nature of breasts is bound to be comfortable.

"Yea, and they have a smell."

A smell????

"My boobs *smell???*" I asked with worry and astonishment.

"Yes," he said simply.

"Like, it's really hot and I've been sweating under my boobs all day smell?"

"It's not a bad smell," he assured me.

I was still not sure I was hearing this correctly. "Like, they smell different than my arm?" I asked.

"Yes," he said. "They have a distinct soft smell. I like it."

This is the first time I've heard about my boob smell. I'm still not sure what to think about it.

As I wrote this, I turned to him and asked playfully "do you want to smell my boobs?" His eyes lit up, a smile instantly spread across his face, and he said "oh yea!" and pulled me close, burying his face in my chest.

I guess I have nothing to worry about.

❈ ❈ ❈

#FREETHENIPPLE

The year was 1997. I was graduating with university degree #1. My parents had come to my grad ceremony in a neighbouring city. I was sitting in the backseat of their car, while they rode in the front. I cracked open my final transcript for the first time. From the backseat I exclaimed "I got an A+ in one of my courses!!"

"Oh yea?" they asked, their interest piqued. "Which class?"

Just as eagerly, I exclaimed "Religion and SEX-U-ALITY!!"

It was one of their proudest moments, I'm sure.

I know what you're thinking- a whole class on religion and sexuality? Yes, that's right. In fact, the university had such thought-provoking religious studies courses that I actually ended up with a minor in religious studies at the end of that 4 year program. This from someone who had never gone to church.

In Religion and Sexuality I had written a kick-ass report that had secured my high mark in the class. In fact, it was the one research paper that I still think about to this day and wish I had kept all these years later. I had boldly dared to tackle the very complicated modern day discourse of nudity and how it has been significantly molded by religion over the ages, namely Christianity. I now realize how little I scraped the surface of such a tangled topic, the social construction of human nudity.

I was very proud of the final product, but I also loved the process of writing that paper. It made me feel so free, so academic and so unoppressed by saying the words "penis" and "vagina" throughout the text. I was unapologetic and unashamed. It was liberating.

* * *

From a very early age, I've thought that the gender double standard was absurd. I noticed girls always seemed to get the short end of the stick. I've been pretty much pissed off about this my whole life. In fact, I'm pretty sure I came out of the womb pissed off about it. When I was a young girl and was excluded from activities based on being a girl, I got very angry. And not just angry- I genuinely couldn't begin to comprehend why I would be excluded because I didn't have a penis. (It's not like the boys *used* their penises to do the activity.) Even more inconceivable to me was that all the other kids didn't seem to question it. Being excluded based on gender wasn't anything I ever accepted, and I certainly didn't accept it into my adulthood.

"Men's only" events don't stop me if I want to attend. It's not that I'm trying to make a statement with this; I genuinely tend to like activities that had often been considered to be more "male" than "female." Making a statement by defying their stupid rule is definitely a bonus though.

I'm also not a fan of "ladies only" activities. Having a uterus doesn't make me enjoy things like bridal showers. I'd rather go shoot something, impale a worm on a hook, or drive a race car.

Another thing that sucks about being a girl (besides not getting invited to all the beer-drinking poker games) is the modesty that has been forced on us. We've been taught (often forced) to be more modest than men.

The ultimate gender double standard when it comes to "modesty"... the nipple.

I subscribe to the school of thought that it's ridiculous that women cannot show their nipples, but men can.

I find the sexualisation of breasts to be both frustrating and fascinating.

At what point does a female's chest become sexualized?

Why is it a man can have more breast tissue than a woman, and they can show their entire breast and nipple, but a woman cannot?

Here is my personal conundrum: even though I feel that not being able to show our nipples is ridiculous, I am indeed a product of social conditioning and I am too modest (embarrassed?) to show mine in public. While one side of me wants to set my breasts free, the other side tells me my boobs are not "perfect", and that they must remain contained in a bra and hidden from public view.

When I breastfed my first daughter, I was initially uncomfortable to nurse her in public. But, I was also (even in my uncomfortableness) extremely stubborn; I wasn't going to be forced to hide the natural process of breastfeeding. I made it a personal mission to push through the discomfort and breastfeed her whenever and wherever she needed to eat. It began to feel less uncomfortable with time. I was proud of my accomplishment, hoping that this somewhat defiant act would make it a bit easier for my children to publicly breastfeed their own children when it became their turn.

Approximately 13 years have passed since my lactating days, and the ta-tas are well locked away. The thought of whipping out a breast to feed an infant is completely foreign to me now.

* * *

Some months ago I was at the mall in another city and entered a clothing store. There was a young, attractive woman working in customer service who helped me, and then began ringing in my purchase. I was caught totally off guard throughout the transaction; she was clearly not wearing a bra.

I'm not sure why this rocked my world so much, but it did. She was in public, at her place of employment, not wearing a bra. It was hard for me not to stare. This was something I never saw. Natural breasts, covered, acting as natural breasts do… uncontained, moving around a bit. It took me awhile to process this. I was confused, shocked, grateful, intrigued. When I left that store, I felt liberated, and it wasn't even me going braless.

Some people might say she wasn't dressed "appropriately." The thing is, there is no law (here) about needing to wear a bra. Her body was well-covered. She had on a form-fitted dress that was very long, sleeveless, and high in the neck area. There was zero visible cleavage.

I'm not sure why, but I felt empowered by this young woman's decision to go braless.

On that same trip in that same city, I noticed this phenomenon repeating on the street as women walked by. It isn't until you see a woman walk briskly past you on the street that you realize how immobilizing a bra is. I tried not to be obvious in my noticing- but there they were- natural breasts, doing what natural breasts do.

I wouldn't be completely truthful if I said public bralessness didn't challenge even my quite liberal views. I liken it to when women wear short shorts, showing the cellulite on their thighs. The questioning in my head becomes seemingly instinctual, but one I know I've been taught to have... *should she be wearing that? Is it appropriate? Can she pull off that look? Does she not care about the cellulite? Why doesn't she wear longer shorts? Shouldn't she be wearing a bra? What do others think about no bra in the workplace? Is this drawing attention?*

Yes, sometimes I catch myself thinking this way. And when I notice myself doing so, I quickly check myself.

I feel like only a small demographic of people are *allowed* to be publicly naked. Social media magnifies how this is so. Recently there was an uproar online about Heidi Klum posting a photo of herself topless. Yes, you can see some nipple in the photo. The Internet went wild and got NASTY.

I understand that many people practice "modesty" and not showing our bodies publicly is part of that. But this was so much more. This was ageism. And probably some other "isms".

What was most obvious to me was that if Heidi were 20 years younger there would have been little backlash. The fact that she is a mother and a wife and is over 45 years of age makes people angry. Even though she still has the body of a 25 year old, it doesn't fit with what people expect of a 40+ mom. By reading the endless opinionated social media comments, one would deduce that mothers who appear topless outside of the home lack respect for themselves and their children, and are exhibiting signs of a midlife crisis.

Well.

※ ※ ※

A brief synopsis of female breast appropriateness:

The female breast is sexual and should be hidden. It can be shown and appreciated if the person is young, but not too young. She must be 18 years of age minimum, but ideally under the age of 30. She should be attractive; her breasts can vary in size, but should be con-

sidered "youthful." If the woman has children she should not show her breasts in any nature that could be perceived as sexual (nursing a baby could be ok, but depends on context). Mothers who show their breasts in a sexual light break an unwritten code and disrespect themselves, and also lose credibility as mothers. If the bearer of the breasts is married, she must not show anyone other than her husband, as they are only for him to see. If she's a grandmother, it doesn't matter what she or her breasts look like- she should be covered from head to toe. If the breast bearer is overweight, she is only allowed to show her bosom in an acceptable venue (such as a known body-positive safe space), otherwise she should be prepared for harsh ridicule.

A crash course in male breast appropriateness:

Males should wear a shirt at work, or when in indoor public spaces such as a shopping mall or a restaurant. His age, relationship status, and fatherhood status are irrelevant in regards to how he should or shouldn't present his manly chest to the world.

❋ ❋ ❋

For as long as I can remember, I have had the illusion that I can somehow WILL things to happen, with some kind of special force that I possess. No, I'm not superstitious. And I'm not delusional (or so I think), so I'm not sure where this comes from.

Well, I was recently driving home with my daughters and we were passing by a casino that is settled just beside a major highway. It was beckoning for me to come in and play, anything other than Keno. We want to build a new family home for our large combined family, and so the lure of a big win pulled me into the parking lot.

I parked. I told the girls that they'd need to waste a few minutes- I was heading into the casino with my 20 dollar bill. I was gonna max bet and win big. That house was mine. I'd be out in just a few minutes.

My daughter took my bankcard and kept it for safekeeping so I had no way to access more funds and lengthen my stay. Smart.

A few things about me that you'll need to now know:

1. I have always looked very young for my age.

2. If I'm trying to look not guilty (even if I'm totally innocent), chances are I'm awkwardly looking guilty.

Before heading in I realized I didn't have my ID because I had recently misplaced it. Of course, I then got paranoid that I would be mistaken for being half my age and they'd ask to see my ID, which I would not be able to provide. Since I had dressed for a car trip not an outing, I looked like a shluppy college student at the time.

"Hmm…" I said before getting out of the car. "I don't have my ID. I need to try to look older."

I thought about this some more and said "maybe I should loosen up my bra straps a bit."

My daughter piped up without missing a beat "just take your bra right off- that should do it."

I've written her out of the inheritance. Well, I would have, had I won anything and had an inheritance to leave to anyone.

SEEING BROWN

A lot of good things come in brown. Chocolate, of course. Chocolate bars... chocolate Easter eggs... chocolate syrup...chocolate ice cream... poop (if you're constipated this is a good thing, believe me)...cinnamon... cinnamon buns... cinnamon pretzel bites, my partner's eyes...

Why isn't brown a more popular clothing color? Maybe it is, but I've just somehow missed the trend. Black is slimming, and brown is close to black, so dark brown must be slimming too, right?

I have owned many pairs of jeans in my lifetime, all of which were not brown. With some courage a few years ago, I did try on a white pair of jeans when I was shopping.

White?

How practical are white jeans? Especially for clumsy and messy people such as myself. Not very practical.

I always feel like by wearing white jeans one is making an announcement to the world that they are currently not having their period. Because wearing white jeans while menstruating is downright crazy.

So, on a non-menstruating day, I tried on white pants in a store. These weren't just any white pants. These apparently were some specially manufactured high tech fabric that was said to repel liquids. I was told that I could spill coffee on these pants and they wouldn't stain (maybe these were designed by women of childbearing age). This point convinced me- I bought them. Yes, a moment of temporary insanity made me buy the white pants.

You might think this risky move was totally out of the blue, but things had been leading up to this point slowly. It unravelled a bit like exposure therapy, how you'd introduce the person to the aversion slowly. In the earlier days of the exposure therapy, I had gone as far as to buy very stretchy, bum-hugging light grey jeans, and another pair that were such a light purple color that they almost looked white at first sight.

But, here's the thing that I hadn't really considered carefully. When I had bought the tight purple pants, I happened to be there at the same time as the ex-wife of a man I was then dating. She's a petite stylish thing. We had gotten along well and I think she appreciated me in her children's lives, so there was Mom Respect there.

Well, she had caught me hemming and hawing in the mirror over those light purple jeans. And I made what was likely a huge mistake- I asked about my butt in the pants, saying that I felt it looked too big. She told me it looked good, and to go ahead and buy the pants.

I know what you're thinking. And obviously one of 3 things happened:

She sincerely thought my butt looked ok and not too big in the jeans.

OR

She didn't give a flying fig about it, and was supportive as women should be with one another and encouraged me to buy and wear whatever the heck I wanted to wear, and not worry about what other people think.

OR

My ass looked huge and awful in the jeans and she took personal satisfaction in knowing I was going to buy and wear them.

I have been wondering since that day if she has been chuckling in her mind about my ill-fated purchase.

Back to the current status of the tight light jeans...

I no longer own the pure white ones. But, it wasn't due to exposure therapy not working.

After watching a few episodes of Netflix's Tidying Up with Marie Kondo, I did a major closet overhaul. The white stain-proof jeans didn't make the cut. In all honesty, the stretch didn't work, the fit wasn't right, and I felt like my ass was 4 feet wide AND flat. With my newly inspired Marie Kondo gratitude, I thanked the pants for serving their purpose in my life, then shoved them into a black garbage bag that was destined for the donation bin. I hope they found their way to a lovely coffee-spilling, menstruating, flat-assed grateful woman.

I did keep the light grey and purple pairs. Yes, my ass looks pretty bountiful in them. They're tight. They hug. I feel like there should be a sign on my back that says "look here" with a downward pointing arrow. Although, in a way I feel like the sign isn't needed because the pants speak for themselves.

However, I've noticed a funny thing the more I put on these pants. I'm really truly starting to not mind my tush. After all, my guy loves it. He thinks it's cute and beautiful. He loves my curves. I know I shouldn't let what a man thinks of my body influence how I feel about my body. A man's opinion should not define my worth. (No one's opinion should define my worth.) However, I do feel different lately. I feel like embracing my body. Embracing my bum. Embracing my curves. Embracing my breasts. And I can say, I'm starting to like them.

The thing is, I know he'd like my body if it were smaller. I know he'd like it if it were bigger. I know he'd like it if it were flatter. He not only loves me but really *likes me*, and by association he loves the body that houses my quirky and playful personality. The body that gave me children that we both love. The body I share with him.

Embracing my body feels GOOD.

Back to the brown. Brown philosophy. Brené Brown, philosophy that is.

Those of us who haven't lived under a rock for the past decade have likely heard of Brené Brown. She gave an incredibly popular Ted Talk in 2010, and many other talks since. She has published 5 New York Times best selling books. Perhaps 6 by the time you are reading this, as I believe she recently released another book.

Brené tackles the very universal human emotions of shame and vulnerability. Despite our tendency to try to avoid shame and vulnerability, much less to talk about it, people are drawn to her work because it resonates with all of us. She has spent over 20 years studying these topics, as well as courage and empathy.

One of the common themes that surfaces particularly with women is that of accepting one's own body, or of *not* accepting it.

My partner and I recently watched the Netflix Original Special called Brené Brown: The Call to Courage, released in 2019. Brené is easy to listen to because she's authentic, charming, funny and tells stories we can relate to. While we were watching that program I had a big a-ha moment.

Brené said, "Like every woman born in this country, I've had to do my share of body image work. And I have- to the point that *I am dangerous*, I like myself so much. Like, I'm good with *everything*."

That's the way I want to live. I want that to be my truth. My dangerously free truth.

❦ ❦ ❦

Chronic pain is an energy suck. It saps your energy to the point that you have to use your limited energy very wisely. You'd be surprised at how much energy it takes to shower, brush out long hair, dress and put on makeup... until you've been in this situation, that is.

There was a time not too long ago that my health was compromised to the point that I wasn't able to wash and brush out my own hair each day. I no longer take being able to do my own basic care for granted.

I frequently see memes online about women having two looks: one being very well put-together, the other being a complete slob. Like so many other women, such is now my life. I either look pretty good, or like I just rolled out of a ditch. Or like the raccoon that spent the night in our compost bin, and was disoriented and almost unrecognizable when I set him free.

On the days that I do look best, the kids come home from school and greet me with a comment which indicates that they've noticed my efforts.

"Oh! You look nice today," offers the first one.

"Yeah," another one pipes up. "Where did you go?"

"Um…" I pause to come up with one of my usual smart-ass remarks, but none come. "Nowhere," I continue. "I showered. And decided to change out of my pajamas."

Being the supportive people that they are, they still look happy for me.

I do still have those days that I'll do errands around town when I'm a super slob. Now that I've hooked the guy of my dreams I don't care about trying to look hot at the grocery store. And I'm not wanting to run into a modelling scout. And I will never be a beauty social influencer. So yeah, why stress about always looking my best.

※ ※ ※

It's Thursday morning. Our alarms have gone off and we are snuggled together, getting that last bit of each other before I have to get the kids up for school and he gets ready for work. We're snuggled right in as usual, legs intertwined, holding each other. He's incredibly warm and I'm too hot, but I can't miss this moment that I love. We are face to face, my cheek pressing up against his eyes, which are closed. Out of courtesy, I'm trying to avoid breathing my morning breath onto him, even though I know he doesn't care.

He says to me, "You're beautiful."

"Huh?"

"You're beautiful, " he says again.

"You can't see me," I acknowledge.

There's a pause...

He clarifies, "Well, you *feel* beautiful."

I know that he is talking about my physical appearance. I also know that he is talking about who I am as a person. All the traits that he finds attractive.

I smile. I have no doubt that I am loved, and that I am beautiful.

A FAMILIAR STRANGER

I stare into my eyes in the mirror. My eyes look hollow, knowing and sad.

I take a hard look at my skin. I see pores and fine lines that I don't usually notice unless there's more natural light. *Maybe I choose not to usually see them*, I think. I see a few spots of acne, which I've become so accustomed to that I no longer give them much thought. I see the deeper wrinkles that have settled into my face, showing my four decades. I see dry skin that lingers despite my futile attempts to exfoliate and moisturize. *I still don't drink enough water*, I think. I see skin that has loosened around my jaw, proof that I am no longer the young woman I once was.

I hold back tears as I take a long, hard look at my face.

I continue to stare back at this person that I somewhat recognize but had never made full peace with. Her eyes soften as they look back at me, telling me *it's ok*.

❈ ❈ ❈

I wait for further testing from medical specialists. Due to unfortunate timing, it will be even further delayed by shutdowns due to Covid-19. The medical establishment is in survival mode right now, and my needs are not priority in the pandemic.

I fully understand and accept this.

There's a part of me that even welcomes this ignorance, staying at home with my family within the safe confines of these walls. Forced isolation gives me an excuse to not get answers. It gives me a legitimate means to hide behind a shroud of denial, one of my best yet most destructive ways of coping. Unfortunately, this shroud doesn't do anything to mask the symptoms I continue to experience. They are cruel reminders that my body is giving up on me, perhaps a lot faster than my mind.

I try to hide some of the symptoms from my partner, not wanting to upset him. But he can feel them and see them. I try to accept my mortality, just in case. I start conversations with him about what I'd like him to do in the future, without me. I want him to go on that dream trip we had planned (now postponed due to the pandemic). I suggest possible designs for his new home with his next wife. It gives me a wee sense of control in a situation I have no control over. But this talk upsets him. He has big plans for the next few years and into our old age, and I am a key part of these plans.

"We'll wait to see what the results are from the swallow study," the doctor had said.

The swallow study got postponed in the pandemic.

"We'll wait to see if you develop any muscle wasting," he had also said.

And so, I wait for the functions of my body to possibly betray me even more than they already have.

❈ ❈ ❈

I feel anger as I look at this person who looks back in the mirror. *Why the hell was I so cruel to her?* But, she returns a look to me that is not anger- it's compassion. She's urging me to fully understand the miracle that is my body.

I look down. I see the "flub" on my belly that came with having children and decided to stay. Why had I ever resented this extra skin? *This is a visible reminder of the 3 beautiful children that I made within my own body*, I say to myself.

I look at my breasts. I nourished my babies with these. *How incredible... I actually made milk*, I say to myself.

I look down to my butt. Even now, with lumps and bumps and cellulite, I smile. There's that dimple. *This butt has served me well*, I say to myself. I've used it for 19 years to hold doors open while I push a stroller or wheelchair in and out of store entrances. It's also provided me with a very comfy cushion.

I look to my thighs, an undeserving long-time recipient of disgust. I realize that they've done what they were supposed to do all along. They provided me with strength to do things I needed to do. They stored fat, as they were meant to. I wasn't intended to have the hard muscular thighs of a man- I have girl thighs. *My girl thighs worked just as perfectly as they should have*, I say to myself.

I look at that woman in the mirror, the entirety of her. Her body is perfect in its imperfection. MY body is perfect in my imperfection. I feel only gratitude for what it's done for me, and what it is still doing for me.

I am reminded of a healthy coping strategy that I've used for quite some time, one that keeps me grounded and keeps things in perspective. When something goes wrong and I'm upset I ask myself "when I'm 90 years old and I look back over my life, will this have mattered? Will I remember it?"

The time I ruined my laptop by spilling water on it... *will I still be upset about that?*

When I was angry at myself because I lost the $100 bill... *did it impact me that much financially?*

Turning my hair greyish green when I was 20... *will that be important then?*

The roll of stubborn flub that peeked out over the purplish jeans I squeezed myself into... *will I really care?*

Maybe I won't live to be an old woman. Maybe I have much less time. The fact is, none of us know how much time we have. So, I ask myself this... *what do I want to remember about my life that is of importance?*

What matters is that I showed up. That I wore the bathing suit and hurled myself down the waterslide. That I laughed until my guts hurt. That I helped teach my daughters the value of respecting themselves. That I had fun when I went bathing suit shopping with my daughter, and got to see her do a little dance when she found the right one. That I found a partner who loves the way I look, and loves who I am inside even more. That my dog doesn't care how big my butt is, as long as I throw her ball and give her kisses on her nose. For the first time, I feel whole.

Lately, I take even more time to touch the soft skin on my son's cheek, and run my fingers gently over that delicate little mole I've always loved. When I kiss my daughter on the top of her head, I take in a slow, deep breath and absorb the scent of her hair. I listen with even more wonder to the comforting sound of my partner's heart beating when I rest my head on his chest. They're the things that matter. I close my eyes and commit that softness, that smell and that steady beat to my memory.

※ ※ ※

When faced with the daunting task of finishing this book, I crumbled during the editing process. This was the article that grew itself into a book, the book that was never meant to be.

Doubt crept in.

My partner had urged me throughout the process to continue writing, knowing that getting the content down was therapeutic. He also nudged me through the editing process, assuring me that my reluctance and doubt was "normal."

But now I was near the end and had hit a wall.

I put down my notes, lamenting out loud. My 17 year old daughter was beside me as I whined and questioned the entire existence of this project.

"Why did I do this? Who is going to read this? I don't want any-

one to read this. *Why did I spend so much time capturing all of this, to not want to share it with anyone???"*

My daughter immediately stopped what she was doing. She turned and looked directly at me, with purpose.

"No, mom," she said gently but sternly. "You have to finish it. It could help someone. Someone needs to hear this story."

It was in that moment that I *knew* that that person, that "someone" was not my daughter. I was filled with pride and relief that she would not struggle to love herself.

So, here it is. My love story. A testament to learning to love my physical body, captured for someone who needed to hear this story. For someone who needed to share a laugh, a cry, or a relatable experience. Maybe that someone is you.

Don't wait to cherish the body you have. Cherish the rolls, the big nose, the stretch marks that make you you. Surround yourself with others who cherish it. Don't settle for less.

ABOUT THE AUTHOR

Jennifer Belyea Ashe

During the first year of her university degrees, Jennifer was asked by a professor "Where did you learn to write?" Thinking he was speaking about her shoddy penmanship, she muddled through an awkward response. She later understood that the question was not about the hurried scribbles on the exam that she had passed in- he was in fact asking about her writing style.

Although she could not write fiction if her life depended on it, she can whip up a well referenced educational resource, a compelling interest article, and an irresistable product review. But where her unique expertise lies is in sharing her own voice.

Jennifer presently (and likely will always) live in cheery Atlantic Canada. She co-exists with her new (and permanent) husband, their five children, an unknown number of (likely dead) plants, a crazy dog, and at least two cats*.

*One daughter is determined to sneak another kitten into the house.